M

D1345024

Moral Literacy

or

How To Do The Right Thing

Colin McGinn

Duckworth

First published in 1992 by
Gerald Duckworth & Co. Ltd.
The Old Piano Factory
48 Hoxton Square, London N1 6PB

A catalogue record for this book is available
from the British Library

ISBN 0 7156 2417 2

Printed in Great Britain by
Redwood Press Ltd, Melksham

Contents

Contents

Preface

Except in the broadest sense, this is not a work of moral philosophy. It is more a work of moral persuasion or advocacy. Philosophical argument sometimes comes into it, but so also do common sense, entreaty, rhetoric, humour – the usual apparatus of ordinary moral conversation. It ranges from the obvious and traditional to the radical and controversial. Sometimes I say things you might not need to hear; at other times I say things you would rather not hear. Like moral discourse in general, it goes from the banal to the exotic, all in the course (and cause) of fixing the moral gaze in what I believe to be the right direction.

I intend this book for readers with no particular interest in academic questions. They just want to figure out right from wrong in a number of different areas, and could use a little guidance. I think of my ideal reader as young and open-minded, not yet hardened into the dogmas that so often beset the later years (of course, you are only as old as the way you think). I invite such readers to enter into a moral dialogue with me: I will say things and they can decide whether they agree or not.

I don't like badness in people; it gives me the creeps. I also don't like moral stupidity; I wish there were less of it. I have the impression sometimes that morality is in some disrepute nowadays, possibly because religion comes harder to people than it used to. People seem not to care about it very much. Some even affect to believe that it is a sham, an illusion. This book is dedicated to opposing that point of view. Morality is real and important, and isn't always self-evident. You have to work at it if you want to get it right.

I suppose I have to confess to wanting to make the world a better place, which is why I have written this book. It is a motive that is hard to suppress, despite its hopelessness. But you never know, do you?

For helpful reactions to an earlier draft, I would like to thank Stephan Chambers, Colin Haycraft, Douglas Husak, Pandora Kazeppis, Consuelo Preti and Michele Schiffer. Let me also thank all the people I have known, good and bad, who have made me think about morality.

New York   C. McG.
December 1991

1

Introduction

I am an academic philosopher by profession: that is how I earn
my living – theoretically. I write books and articles on abstruse
philosophical topics, and I teach students about these topics. I
confess to finding abstract philosophical questions extremely
interesting. So I have devoted a large part of my life to thinking
about them.

But people frequently object to this: they complain that
philosophers like me fail to wrestle with the real questions that
bother ordinary people, thus falling down in their intellectual
duty. They say that philosophers should be concerned, at least
some of the time, with the practical question of How to Live.
Philosophy should tell us – *all* of us – how we should and
shouldn't act, and what values to live by. It should provide moral
guidelines. Philosophers are supposed to have wisdom, after all,
and wisdom is what you need in order to do the right thing.
Philosophers, then, should use their wisdom in more relevant
and practical ways.

I actually sympathise with this complaint. Philosophers really
should, at least *some* of the time, apply their special skills to
practical moral problems. These problems are very important,
and philosophical skills can be extremely useful in dealing with
them. They shouldn't be left to priests and pundits and politicians. And philosophers should try to write about them in ways
that are intelligible without special training. That is what this
book sets out to do. It treats a number of basic moral questions
that confront, or may confront, almost everybody almost every

day. These are questions that can't be avoided, and you need to have some worked-out opinion about them. You need to figure out where you stand, if possible *before* you do the wrong thing. Should you be eating the piece of veal your mother has cooked for you? What ought you to do if you accidentally get pregnant? When is violence a justifiable response to what somebody else does to you? What kind of sexual conduct should you engage in? Which drugs, if any, should you take? Should anyone ever be prevented from saying or publishing certain things? What kind of person is it best to be? These are the kinds of question I shall be discussing – specific, practical, troubling questions. How you answer them determines how you will live your life.

While some people complain that philosophers don't apply themselves enough to concrete moral questions, others may object that it is arrogant and misguided of a philosopher to go around telling other people what to do. By what right do I stand in moral judgement over others? People should be able to make up their own minds about moral matters. Morality isn't the kind of thing in which you can have special expertise, so my opinion is no better – and may be worse – than the next person's. So I should stick to my theoretical interests and leave morality to those of a more worldly bent.

This protest is partly right but also partly wrong. It is partly right because I can't expect you to take anything from me on authority. There is no specialised knowledge I possess which, if only you could understand it, would cause you to agree with me. It is not that philosophers have recently made some startling moral discoveries that lay people have to take on trust. Moral truths are not like the truths of theoretical physics. But I have no intention of pulling anything like that on the reader. What I propose to do is put forward various considerations, offer my assessment of them, and then invite you to agree (or disagree) with what I conclude. You won't be asked to accept anything that you yourself cannot see to be correct. In a way, it is all just common sense. My justification for writing this book is that, as a philosopher, I have had a lot of practice in thinking about conceptual questions, questions of principle – which is what philosophers are supposed to be good at. I have also thought quite a bit about the particular issues to be discussed, for one reason or another. Let the proof of the pudding be in the eating: if you don't find what I say clear or helpful or illuminating, then I have failed and should keep to metaphysics; if you do, then the project of writing this book is not a mere impertinence.

I heard of a mathematician who wrote a popular mathematics book because it pained him to see people constantly committing mathematical fallacies in everyday life, particularly in matters of probability, thus getting themselves into sticky situations. He felt that, as a professional mathematician, he might have something useful to offer. To achieve his aim it was necessary to make the relevant mathematical ideas as clear and intelligible to his lay reader as possible. Well, my aim in this book is not a million miles away from that distressed mathematician's. It pains me to see people making ethical mistakes, in daily life as well as in politics, thus getting themselves (and others) into sticky situations and worse. If only they could think more clearly! That is why I decided, quixotically, to write a book for the general reader that might help remedy this sad state of affairs. The mathematician's interest was numerical literacy, mine is moral literacy. As I said, you are to be the judge of whether I have anything useful to contribute to this cause.

The approach I shall follow seeks to replace taboo morality with rational morality. Taboo morality tells you what to do and what not to do simply as a matter of decree. Certain things are deemed simply *taboo* and that is an end to it. Maybe some god or other authority has declared that the thing in question is taboo; in any case, no *reason* is given for the moral prohibition. 'Thou shalt not eat cabbage on Wednesdays'—that type of thing. Rational morality, by contrast, seeks to give reasons for its judgements and prohibitions; nothing has to be taken on faith, as simply *so*. If an adequate reason can't be given, then this is admitted and the prohibition dropped or at least held in suspicion. My method, then, will be that of argumentative persuasion, not threat or admonition or incantation. My aim is to *convince* you of certain things, not to make you think or do what happens to suit me, by hook or by crook. This is to be a meeting of minds, not an assertion of will. Inner assent is what I am interested in.

Some people may scoff at the idea of rational morality. Don't I know that morality isn't rational, that it has no real objectivity? I speak as if there were such a thing as moral truth! Really, it will be said, morality is relative and subjective, just so much emotional sounding-off. It is what you use to keep the kids quiet.

Well, actually, yes, I am afraid I do believe in the idea of moral truth, and I don't think morality is relative in any sense that would undermine my project in this book. But I don't want to get into this kind of abstract question here – my aims are more particular and practical. I simply invite you to read the book, think about it, and decide if you agree or disagree with what I say about specific issues. Forget big questions like Relativism versus Absolutism – that's just philosophy.

However, I can't resist making a couple of quick points about the kind of flabby relativism in which some people nowadays claim to believe. First, I really *do* think that (say) Hitler's acts of genocide were morally wrong, horribly so, no matter what anyone happens to believe on the matter – and so, I think, do you. We don't think the concentration camps were wrong merely 'from our current perspective' or some such thing. I don't care if the whole world suddenly decides, in a fit of insanity, that it was all morally fine; I don't even care if nobody ever believed it was wrong: *it was still wrong*. For the wrongness does not depend on anybody's believing it was wrong, any more than the existence of dinosaurs depends on anyone believing in them. Similarly, I believe – and I bet you do too – that inflicting unnecessary pain on someone against their will is wrong in itself, independently of what people happen to believe on the subject. Acts are not *made* right or wrong simply by people believing that they are right or wrong. This is pretty obvious really, though some people will keep saying things that seem to ignore it.

Secondly, relativists are often shrilly moralistic in their defence of relativism: they think that moral absolutism is a bad view, encouraging intolerance and so on. But I ask them: is absolutism itself only bad in a relative way – only wrong for them and not necessarily for others? If so, then it might not be wrong for me – I can believe in it and act on it. On the other hand, if it is wrong for everybody, then it is abolutely wrong – which contradicts the relativist's position. So moral relativism is either self-refuting or it has no claim on my moral beliefs. In either case, I don't need to take it seriously. This is, I know, a 'philosophical' argument against crude relativism, but it is an argument which neatly exposes the logical absurdity of the view. It is like saying that there is no reason to believe anything and forgetting to ask whether this also is something we should believe. Anyway, as I said, I don't want to get too involved in these abstract questions here; so let's put this behind us and concentrate on the concrete issues. They are where the real moral action is.

A less abstract preliminary question concerns morality and religion. Although I won't be appealing to divine revelation or command in this book, I don't intend my conclusions to be anti-religious. Rather, I mean to be neutral on religious questions, in the sense that both theists' and atheists will be addressed. But I should state what I take the relation between morality and religion to be. Many people believe that morality has its basis in God's commands. They think that God decides what is right and what is wrong, thereby *making* morality be what it is. They also believe, or fear, that without God morality could have no basis or justification.

This position has a superficial appeal, but it is decisively refuted by an argument that goes back to Plato. The argument is very simple; and it shows that genuine moral rules could not be *created* by God's will. First, ask whether God could make what we now think is wrong right. Could He, by divine command, decide that murder is right after all, thus making it right from now on? This seems an odd question: how can you *make* something that was wrong right just by declaring it to be so? It is like making something false true just by saying that it is true. God can't do that, and if He could we would have every reason to distrust His edicts. How can we respect God's moral law if it represents nothing but His arbitrary whim? So presumably God can't just invent goodness by brute assertion; rather, we must assume, His nature is to decree what *is* good – independently of His *decreeing* it to be so. But then God doesn't literally *make* things good; He simply recognises that certain things *are* good and then judges us according to our conformity to this. God judges that a murderer did something wrong because murder *is* wrong and God (being omniscient) knows that; it is not that murder gets to be wrong because God happens to *judge* that it is. Even God couldn't make murder right simply by judging it to be so. So God's decrees are not the ultimate source of moral truth; they are the recognition of a prior moral reality – which is, indeed, why His decrees should be respected. To put it differently: even if there were no God murder would still be wrong; adding God to the picture can't change this moral fact. So atheists (like myself) have no good excuse for refusing to take morality seriously.

That was another rather abstract general argument, which I am trying to keep to a minimum so as not to lose the moral trees to the wood. What I am anxious to stress is that we should do our moral thinking with the same organ we use for other kinds of thinking, namely the head. We should use our reason, not our prejudices or our faith or our parents or our society. Emotions can come into it, but they shouldn't be allowed to run away with our brains – as so often happens in moral argument and debate. A warm heart and a cool head is the best combination here. You mustn't let the temperature of the former determine the contents of the latter. Use your intelligence, in a word. Stay calm.

I hope I strike a chord in the cool warmth of my reader when I say that *freedom* is a good thing. People should be free, they shouldn't be coerced. They should be allowed to pursue their interests and desires and dreams, not curbed and frustrated and held back. What this value of freedom comes down to is simply that people should be allowed to do what they want – other things being equal, of course. And here is where morality steps in. People should be free to do what they want, so long, that is, as it is not morally wrong. I should be free to eat bananas if I want to, but I shouldn't be free to shoot people at random just because I feel like it.

Morality thus fixes limits to personal freedom: limits to what desires you can legitimately satisfy. Basically, it is a set of rules for harmonising what I want to do with what is good for others. Taking what is yours, for example, may give me what I want, but it won't do you any good: hence theft is wrong. In any particular case, a debate about what it is permissible for me to do is a debate about the respects in which my freedom to act should be limited. Therefore, moral prescriptions inherently conflict with a positive value, the value of personal freedom.

There can be no denying or dodging this basic fact: morality exists precisely to thwart your freedom to act on your selfish desires. That is why we often don't want to do what we should do. Morality consists in restrictions on our freedom. And since freedom is itself a good, morality inherently involves a conflict of goods. Thus, in a sense, there is always something bad about any good act. Someone is always not getting what he wants. We shouldn't restrict people's freedom unless we really have to, but if we don't bad things will result – other people's freedom will be restricted. So we can think of moral questions as questions about how much it is reasonable to restrict people's freedom to do as they like – that is, how much frustration should be imposed on the individual for the sake of a greater good.

That is the general nature of morality, which is why people don't always conform to it and why it is often tempting not to. It can be tough, I know, doing what's right, but that is the make-up of the beast. Most of the questions discussed in this book will have this form, as we shall soon see. We shall constantly be assessing the rival claims of personal freedom, on the one hand, and moral restraint, on the other. To be free or not to be free: that is the moral question. In a way, then, this book is about how much freedom people ought to have, assuming that they can't have total freedom – human desires being what they all too commonly are. It is not all going to be good news for the selfish ego. The ego can't always get what it wants. But there is something weightless and spongelike about unlimited freedom, is there not? It is possible to relish the constraints on action that morality imposes. Morality is the gravity of the will, what keeps our feet on the ground.

We shall soon be getting down to concrete cases, but general introductions have to be indulged, however tedious. They set the scene and tone: they are the map we need to consult before we can get out there and discover things. And there is one other thing about my general method that you may need warning about: the use of imaginary hypothetical examples. Don't think this takes us away from the real world into irrelevant fantasy land – the philosopher's vice. The purpose of these imaginary examples is not distraction but focus, focus on the essential. By means of them we can disentangle the factors that bear on our moral assessments, test our principles, and come to a clearer view of the actual case in hand. Often a moral view of some actual case is defended on the basis of a principle that can be seen to be unacceptable by considering a slightly different hypothetical case. These imaginary examples shed light on the real world by directing our attention to features of our practices that we tend to ignore. This should become clear later in particular applications. Moral reasoning requires the use of the imagination if it is to get results – which is one reason why works of art can be morally enlightening. Imaginative skill is part of moral skill.

Although in what follows I shall be defending specific moral claims, sometimes quite firmly, my real aim is less to induce the same convictions in the reader than to encourage a certain way of thinking about moral questions. It is less *what* you think than the *way* you think it that concerns me – at least in part. It is a question of mental attitude, of approach. I want to impart a certain kind of skill or method – the ability to read a moral problem, to know how to handle it, what considerations to bring in. I want to foster the capacity of 'moral intelligence' as much as, or more than, a specific set of moral beliefs. Thoughtfulness, if you will. If you finish this book with a totally opposite set of moral beliefs to mine, but with an enhanced capacity to articulate and justify your moral position, I will be happy. Fanaticism and stupidity are the two great evils of the world: once these are undermined people can communicate and often converge in what they believe, or at least live with their disagreements. Moral knowledge is not in itself very intellectually difficult to achieve – nothing like as hard as learning calculus or French – and it is really only prejudice and vested interest and laziness that stand in its way. It is a skill that can be learned and refined without undue exertion. But, like driving, it is a skill that everybody thinks they have to perfection without having to pay the matter much attention. So allow me to be your back-seat driver for a while. Put your moral engine into gear, then, and we can take to the open road...

2

Animals

Let us start with animals – other animals. This is a good place to start because the moral issues raised by animals are a powerful illustration of what a rational morality can lead to. Just by thinking about the issue in a critical and impartial spirit you can, I believe, arrive at a radical revision in the way other species are normally regarded. You can cut through a good deal of confused nonsense and harmful prejudice. In addition, animals raise in a sharp way many of the basic issues that arise in the other areas we shall be discussing: issues of harm, freedom, impartiality, unreasonable discrimination, the balancing of interests. We shall see that there is actually a lot wrong with what we do to animals without reflecting on it, and in the way we habitually conceive our moral relation to them.

On the one hand, then, we have the human species – those featherless bipeds with the big brains. On the other hand, in the blue corner, there is the rest of nature – the minerals, the plants, the beasts. We humans need the rest of nature in order to live and thrive. We need to eat some of it, breathe some of it, wear some of it, burn some of it, live in some of it, and so forth. (We are also curious about it and can sometimes appreciate its beauty.) In order to meet our needs, we put nature to our use – we 'exploit' nature. There is no way round this, and there is nothing bad about the exploitation of nature in itself – all animals must do it, as must plants. We hew rock to make houses, cut down trees to make furniture, kill animals for food and clothes. We take from nature what we want – a piece of slate, a branch, a skin. We tend to assume that this is all much the same kind of thing; we are just using what comes to hand for our own benefit, be it mineral, vegetable or animal. We use the not-us for the good of us. Now, the queston is: is there anything wrong with any of this? Are some kinds of exploitation of nature immoral? Do we in fact make the kinds of moral distinctions in nature that it objectively requires us to make?

If you want to know whether some kind of action is right or wrong, then you have to ask how it is for the thing on the receiving end of the action. You can't just look at how *you* feel, what *you* get out of it; you have to consider how *it* feels, the consequences of your action for *it*. You must examine the impact of your action on the things it affects. Now, in the case of rock-quarrying and house-building, there doesn't seem to be any moral issue here: the rock doesn't care what you do to it, because it doesn't have any cares at all – it is just a *rock*. Technically speaking, it is not 'sentient' – it doesn't feel anything, see anything, know anything. It is not even dead, since it was never alive. In the case of a tree, we are at least dealing with something living – something that grows, reproduces, dies, sickens, flourishes, ingests. But we are still not dealing with anything sentient, any more than seaweed is sentient or the mould that grows on rotting food. There is no conscious awareness in the tree. (Yes, I know that some eccentrics have claimed to find evidence of sentience in plants; no doubt there are other eccentrics who are convinced that rocks entertain profound thoughts – let us forget them and stick to common sense.) So we need not worry that the lumberjack's saw operates as an instrument of torture for the felled tree.

But, of course, in the case of animals like cows and dogs and monkeys the same actions would produce immense pain. I leave you to imagine the pain that would be caused to a cow if you took a chainsaw to it – if you treated its neck and legs like the trunk and branches of a tree. Stepping on a tree's root is thus not like stepping on a cow's foot. How does this difference of potential effect bear on the morality of felling or pruning a cow? Is there a moral distinction that goes with the difference in sentience?

This question is not hard to answer. Suppose a man first fells a tree to make a chair and then fells a cow to make a coat: he applies his saw in the same way on one living thing and then on the other, whistling as he works. The tree is killed but suffers no pain, the cow is killed and suffers great agony. The first act was not wrong, the second is a paradigm of cruelty – the man shouldn't have done it. If he needed to kill the cow for a coat, he should at least have done it painlessly – he shouldn't simply have ignored the cow's pain. In short, he shouldn't have treated the sentient thing in the same way he treated the insentient one. What he did was morally wrong. And suppose we learn that he already had a coat or that he could have made an equally good one from cotton: then we think his painful killing of the cow was doubly wrong, was really quite inexcusable. We think this because we make a basic distinction within the class of natural things that we exploit: we distinguish between the things that have no interests and feelings of their own, and the things that do have interests and feelings. We thus think it matters morally to what you do to an object that it feels pain as a result of your action. So we condemn cruelty to animals, and rightly so. An animal isn't a mere *thing*. You can't do just anything to an animal and expect to be regarded as a moral person. Animals restrict your freedom, in that you are not morally free to treat them in any way you feel like treating them. People shouldn't be free to torture animals because they are in a bad mood. Animals constitute a moral limit on human action; they have moral worth or weight.

I assume that what I have just said will strike you as obvious and banal. Whoever thought the opposite? Don't civilised societies have laws protecting animals from wanton cruelty? Yes, it is totally obvious and not in itself a revolutionary point of view. But it raises the big question of how far the underlying principles should be taken. How *much* of human freedom should be sacrificed for the sake of the interests and well-being of animals? What is to count as 'wanton cruelty'? How consistent are we in taking to its logical conclusion the moral standpoint we take as obvious when spelled out as above? Is there, in particular, any conflict between what we thus take as obvious and what we routinely do to animals when we eat them, experiment on them, use them in sport, put them in zoos and circuses, use them as transportation devices, and so on? Are we really balancing their interests against our own in a just and decent way? We can all agree that you shouldn't chainsaw the conscious living cow for the fun of it; but should you put a bolt through its head so that you can cut it up and eat cooked bits of its dead body? Why is the first act generally thought very wrong and the second not? That is where the issue becomes a little more disturbing.

To gain some perspective on the question, let us make use of a couple of imaginary examples of the kind I mentioned in the previous chapter. We will first see what we think about them and then ask whether this is consistent with the orthodox way of thinking about humans and other species.

So: we have all seen those vampire films, creepy tales of powerful pale predators who live on human blood. Well, let me tell you a story about a particularly successful vampire species. This species is unusual among the run of vampires in that it can live equally well off human blood or orange juice. It is also more in control of its food supply than your average vampire. In addition to producing ample supplies of orange juice, it keeps throngs of humans locked up in huge prisons so that it can get to their necks with minimum effort. The vampires raise human infants in these prisons for the sole purpose of drinking their blood at maturity (and they have been known to do it at tenderer ages too). There is a bit of a snag, though, from the vampires' point of view, namely that you can't drink blood from the same human more than three times without that human's dying, so they are continually needing to replenish their stocks as thrice-bitten humans die off. The humans are powerless to resist because of the superhuman capacities of the vampires. When the vampires aren't dining on human blood (and the occasional glass of orange juice) they do the usual civilised things: go to the movies and the opera, make love, get married, play tennis, whatever.

They also have strict laws governing conduct within their species and are generally law-abiding and polite. They are actually not such a bad lot, generally considered, apart from this human blood business. But they don't see much a problem about that because, after all, we humans belong to a different species from them and look and act differently; anyway they have been doing it for millennia. They sometimes think it is a pity about the pain and fear the humans feel while their necks are being punctured and drained, not to mention all the death that results, but there is no point in being squeamish and sentimental about your farm animals, is there? And yes, they could live just as well on orange juice – which they actually rather enjoy at breakfast time – but it would be a little monotonous to have only that to drink: they like some variety in their diet. True, also, it would be healthier to give up human blood, as some of them are always tediously insisting, but they relish their pint of blood at dinner time and feel that life would be poorer without it. So they don't take much notice of the 'juicetarians' among them, a small minority anyhow, who fitfully campaign for humane treatment for humans – and even go so far as to call for complete human liberation! Why, what would become of all the humans if they were set free to roam the land? No, it is inconceivable.

I don't know about you but I find this vampire species a pretty selfish, blinkered and cruel bunch. They have got their values all wrong. If I were a powerful Martian visiting earth and found it dominated by these bloodsuckers, with the human species reduced to the status of mere blood vats, I would insist that they damn well stick to orange juice. Variety, freedom, tradition – don't give me that! Just look what you are *doing* to these poor humans, the pain and misery and confinement you cause them – and all because you don't fancy orange juice all the time. I mean, honestly, are you really telling me that it is morally acceptable to put that child to a slow and painful death rather than squeeze a couple of oranges? Can the difference of taste be that important to you? Human liberation! That is what I would say; and if I were one of the unlucky human victims I would plead the same case, hoping to appeal to the vampires' moral sense – of which they seem to have plenty when it comes to the welfare of their *own* species.

Here is another example, in which the human role is reversed.

Imagine that there are two humanlike species not one, either naturally evolved or created by God, rather as there are a number of monkey species. We are in the dominant position relative to the other humanlike species – call it the 'shuman' species. Shumans, like humans, are intelligent, sensitive, social, civilised – in fact very much on a par with humans in their level of development. However, their warlike prowess is much inferior to ours, and as a result they have been conquered and tyrannised by the 'superior' species. Not content merely with enslaving them to do our dirty work, we also use them for food, as subjects of vivisection experiments and in bloodsports. Our exploitation of them gives us a higher standard of living than we would have otherwise. Their flesh is excellent when barbecued; medical science has progressed rapidly by using them instead of lower species which are biologically less like us; and it is jolly amusing to watch them running away from, and being caught by, the starved dogs we let loose on them on Saturday afternoons. Of course, the shumans complain all the time about what we humans do to them, always petitioning the government from their special reservations, trying to work up some emotional sympathy, causing trouble in the streets. We are not impressed, though, because they belong to another species from ours: we can't interbreed with them, they are completely hairless with pointy ears, and the mothers carry the babies for twelve months not nine. Admittedly we don't *need* to use them in this way – we already have plenty of other species to depend on, as well as the vegetable kingdom – but it can't be denied that we derive pleasure from them that we wouldn't enjoy without exploiting them as we do. So you see it is all right to ignore their interests in order to cater to ours. We don't need to *balance* their interests with ours, treating similar interests equally, since the shumans belong to a different biological group from us. The biological distinction cancels the moral commitments we would have with respect to the interests of members of our own species.

Again, I maintain that this isn't right. We are doing to them what the vampires were doing to us – trampling over the legitimate interests of another group. In essence, we are refusing to take their welfare seriously simply because they belong to a different biological species from us – *and this difference does not warrant that refusal.* There is a word for this attitude, coined about twenty years ago, namely 'speciesism'. It was coined on analogy with the concepts of racism and sexism, and is intended to suggest that what is morally irrelevant or insignificant – species or race or sex – is being treated as if it carried decisive moral weight. The point of my two imaginary examples is to demonstrate that speciesism *as such* is a form of unacceptable discrimination. There is no good moral defence of what the vampires do to us or what we do to the shumans, and to try to base one on a mere difference of species is transparent special pleading. It is simply quite unconvincing as a justification for what looks on the surface like a naked exercise of power designed to benefit one group at the ruthless expense of another. Cruelty is cruelty is cruelty – and a mere difference of species doesn't make it right. Ditto for murder, imprisonment, and so on.

The question we must then ask, returning now to the real world, is whether our actual treatment of animals is founded on a tacit speciesism – that is, whether we could rationally condone it if it weren't for mere species differences. Do we, in other words, accord mere zoological distinctions too much weight in deciding what to do and not do to animals? Is the speciesist attitude the only thing that sustains our exploitative treatment of other species? Could we defend this treatment without reliance upon naked species bias?

Once this question is clearly raised, it is very hard to avoid the answer that we do rely, unacceptably, on speciesist assumptions. What tends to obscure this fact is that animals differ from us not *only* in point of what species they belong to; they differ, also, mentally, in terms of their cognitive abilities. They don't have our intellects, our brain power, our moral sense. Their minds are just not as rich and complicated as ours.

But it is easy to see that *this* difference cannot make the moral difference we tend to take for granted – unless, that is, we are prepared to set up a new and pernicious form of social discrimination: 'intelligenceism.' Surely we don't think that mere inferiority of intelligence (by some possibly arbitrary standard) is enough to justify, say, slaughtering the intellectually inferior for food or electrically shocking them for scientific purposes. If we did believe that, we would have the freedom to do these things to human children, mentally backward adults, and senile old people. Indeed, there would be no moral objection to intentionally raising genetically engineered 'simple' humans for such purposes. But being intelligent is not what gives you the right not to be abused. The reason it is wrong to cause pain to people is not that they are intelligent or members of the human species. It is that pain hurts, it is bad to suffer it, people don't like to be in pain. If you want to know whether an action is wrong, you have to look at its actual effects and ask if they are bad for the thing being acted on – not ask what *else* happens to be true of the thing. If forced confinement, say, is bad *for* an animal, then it is bad to do this *to* an animal, unless you can think of a reason why this badness is justifiable in the light of a greater good. It isn't a question of the animal's ability to do mathematics or appreciate chamber music – still less of its species *per se*. It is a matter of sentience, the ability to suffer.

And here we reach the nub of the issue about our moral treatment of animals. *Is* there a greater good that justifies what, considered in itself, appears to be bad? Can we argue that what is bad for the animal is overridden by what is good for us? Is it possible to defend something bad in itself by claiming that the ends justify the means? Note, now, that we are assuming that our treatment of animals would be morally wrong if it were *not* for some supposed greater good.

A clear-eyed look at the facts quickly reveals that there is no such means-end justification, at least in the vast majority of cases. The test to use here is whether you would condone a given form of treatment if it were practised on humans, thus eliminating the speciesist bias from your deliberations. You may also consider 'simple' humans in order to eliminate intelligenceist bias. That is, you have to ask whether you would do to intellectually comparable humans what we regularly do to animals. I won't bother to run through the whole gamut of things we do to animals, leaving this as an exercise for the reader; once the principle has been grasped this is fairly mechanical work. But it must be clear enough already that you would not condone killing humans for food in the way we now do animals, or experimenting on humans as we now do on animals, or using them in sports as we do now, or using their skins for clothes as we do now, and so on. You wouldn't even do these things to humans who were mentally *inferior* to the animals in question. The pain, the fear, the frustration, the loss of life – these would be quite enough to deter you. And the reason for these sound moral judgements is simply that the ends do *not* justify the means. A life lost for a pleasant taste gained? Mutilation for some possibly trivial increase in knowledge? Dismemberment in the jaws of dogs for the 'thrill of the chase'? Trapped and skinned for an expensive fur coat? We would never accept these calculations if humans constituted the means, so why should we suddenly change our standards when we move outside the human species? Only, it seems, because of the prejudice that declares our species sacred and other species just so much exploitable stuff. Unfair discrimination, in other words.

So what should be done, now that we have seen our treatment of other species for what it is – immorally benefiting ourselves at the expense of other animals? (Actually, it is more that we *think* we are benefiting ourselves, since a lot of what we get from them is bad for us.) We should, at the very least, do everything we can to minimise our dependence on animals, treating their interests as comparable to the interests of fellow humans in the respects relevant to the case at hand. This will mean, just for starters, stopping eating meat if you live in one of the societies in which it is perfectly possible to find other sources of food, i.e. almost everywhere on earth. Don't even think about owning a fur coat. Very few animal experiments, if any. Bloodsports – give me a break. In sum, we have to cease doing to animals what we would not in good conscience do to humans. We must make our morality consistent.

You ask: if it is so wrong, why do people do it? Good question. To answer it, a glance back at history helps. It is a sad fact about human affairs that power tends to rule, and this includes our relation to the animal world. Nor is power always, or indeed often, on the same side as justice. If A is more powerful than B, and A can get something off B which B may not want to give to A, then A is apt to take that something from B by brute force – unless A is a just and moral individual, which he very often isn't. People all too often do what they have the power to do, and to hell with morality. Whenever you have imbalances of power, and a relation of domination that serves one party not the other, then be on the look-out for the kinds of prejudice and ideology that sustain basically immoral arrangements.

Historically, two areas of intense and terrible exploitation stand out, both of which were 'justified' by all manner of strange doctrines at the time: slavery and child labour. I need not review these familiar stories of human brutality and moral blindness, since they are now accepted as such, though it is easily forgotten how recently young children were put through unspeakable miseries in supposedly civilised countries like England and slavery was legally permitted in America. My point is that at the time, and for hundreds of years before, these forms of subjuga-tion were widely taken for granted and not regarded as morally dubious. Only now, in enlightened retrospect, do we wag the finger of condemnation at our forebears and marvel at their moral insensitivity. But which of us alive now can be sure that we would have been on the side of the angels had we lived in those benighted days? The pressures of conformity and self-in-terest and sheer inertia are very strong. May it not now be the case that our treatment of animals, so redolent of the barbarities of slavery and child exploitation, is just one more example of brute power holding sway over natural justice – of self-interest stifling moral decency? But, as with those other cases, it is not always easy to see this when it is all around you. You tend to think it must have *some* justification, even if you can't produce one. But maybe it just doesn't.

There are a great many replies that people make to the case for animal liberation that I have been presenting. I haven't the space (or the inclination) to go through them all here. They range from the religious to the economic, the mystical to the pragmatic. It is usually fairly easy to see through them if you keep the basic moral point firmly in focus – the point that insists

on equal consideration of equivalent interests. Nearly always, it
is the speciesist bias that lurks behind the objection. It suffices
to bring this into the open. My aim here has been to get to the
moral root of the question, not to explore all the ramifications
that arise. Think hard about that first, and then move on to the
complexities and qualifications.

The issue of our duties to animals should be separated from
the issue of our duties to the environment, important as both
issues are. There are, indeed, excellent reasons for criticising
the human relationship to the environment: pollution, deple-
tion, the ruin of natural beauty, and so forth. Part of this
environmental concern is the preservation of animal species.
But these issues are taken to refer back to humans and their
offspring: we are making the environment too unhealthy or
unpleasant for human flourishing, ours and our children's. Now
I have every sympathy for the environmentalist cause, and in
particular for the insistence that we care about the well-being
of the people to come – the unborn generations. But it would
be a distortion to assimilate the morality of our treatment of
animals to this other issue. The question about animals is not
whether it is bad for *humans*, presently existing or to come in
the future, to treat animal populations in the way we do; the
question I have been discussing is whether it is bad for *them*.
Our duty is to them as ends in themselves, not as means to our
ends – such as our contemplation of a rich and beautiful animal
kingdom. The value attaching to animal well-being is not a kind
of instrumental value for human well-being (though there is
that value too); it is a value that derives from their own nature
and imposes duties on us that, so to speak, stop with them. Only
confusion can result from lumping these two kinds of issue
together. Indeed, it is a pernicious confusion, because it sees
everything in terms of human interests, when the whole point
is that there are other interests on earth to be taken into
account. Really, we should be saving the environment for ourselves *and* for the other animals who have to live in it – and who
played no part in its ruin.

People sometimes ask me, accusingly, whether I am an 'ani-
mal-lover'. They want to know whether this is why I think we

owe animals more consideration than we customarily give them. I suppose these people think that my heart beats with infatuation when I see a rat or a spider, or that I prefer animals to humans, or that I have lots of cuddly pets. But that isn't the point at all. The point isn't about love, in any ordinary sense – it is about something closer to respect. It is about independence, freedom, due consideration, equality, rights. In a broad sense, it is about opportunity, the right to live the life that nature has given you without unnecessary interference from outsiders. In much the same way, though children should obviously be loved by some, they should be respected by all, because respect is the attitude that feeds directly into moral esteem. In neither case should powerlessness be taken as an excuse for immoral exploitation. One of the chief functions of morality is the protection of the vulnerable.

In a deeper and more abstract sense, the point also concerns objectivity – seeing the world as it really is and not only from your particular point of view, with your interests and needs taking up all the foreground. We need to be able to think objectively in all moral matters, but in the case of animals the need is especially acute. Always remember: their existence is not an existence for us.

3
Abortion

There is only one way for a human female to become pregnant, namely by the fertilisation of her egg by the sperm of a human male, but there are a great many circumstances in which this can happen. Some of these circumstances are happy for all concerned: both parents wish to have a child at that time, the child will grow up healthy and normal, she will be well-cared for, and no one else will suffer as a result. In these circumstances, no one will consider abortion, nor should they. Even the great pessimists of human life (Arthur Schopenhauer, Woody Allen) stop short of recommending abortion in *every* case, as they stop short of suggesting suicide for all, or interpreting murder as a kind of favour. Human life may not be all that great, but it is usually good enough to be considered worth living.

But the circumstances surrounding conception and pregnancy are not always so happy. The parents may be teenage sweethearts unprepared for the responsibilities of parenthood. Or they may be ships that pass in the night, with no thought of a long-term relationship in mind. Worse, the mother-to-be could be a victim of rape, and the father in prison for raping her; the father could even be *her* father. It might be that the foetus has a severe medical defect, mental or physical, which would make its life and that of the mother and father unrelieved misery, only for the child to die at an early age. Pregnancy can occur in tragic circumstances, in which we would all say that it would have been better if it had never happened: if only contraception had done its work! In these kinds of cases, people frequently think of abortion, and often carry it out, legally or illegally. The question for this chapter is whether abortion is morally permissible and if so in what circumstances. How should we think about this question in order to arrive at the best moral position? What are the key considerations? What, fundamentally, is the question *about*?

I don't think we shall get very far if we insist on defining the issue in terms of whether it is ever right to kill the unborn, as if merely being located inside the mother were the essential point. As it happens, human organisms spend the first nine months of life incarcerated inside the mother's body, but they could have spent three months or two weeks or five years – that is all just accidental biology. What matters to the abortion issue isn't *where* the foetus is when it is killed but *what* it is: its stage of biological and mental development, not its spatial location.

If this is not already obvious, consider the following. Suppose a foetus is scheduled to be aborted on a certain day but the mother gives birth prematurely so that the baby is now outside the mother's body on the day in question and still alive. Is it now suddenly wrong to do what would have been acceptable if the baby had stayed longer inside her? After all, there has been no intrinsic change *in the baby*; it has just gone from one place to another. Or suppose, hypothetically, that human children and adults needed periodically to re-enter the womb – say, every three years for five days – or else they sicken and die, so that the initial stage of motherhood had to be repeated for (say) the first thirty years of a human's life. You come out but you have to go back in again every now and then, for Womb Replenishment. Could it be that killing a fine young man when he is outside the womb counts as the most heinous of crimes and yet becomes morally acceptable for the five days he spends holed up in the mother? Surely, that would be absurd. It would be just as much a case of murder during the interior phase as during the exterior phase, simply because there has been no change *in* the person, only a change in where he is spending his time. So we can't adopt the simple principle, 'inside the mother killing is acceptable, outside it is to be prohibited'. What we have to consider is the *time* at which abortion is contemplated, not the place.

This point shows that we won't focus on the right question if we try to settle the issue by invoking a woman's right over her own body, where this includes any individual who might be inside it. Clearly, you cannot make murder right simply by arranging for it to occur to the victim while he is inside your body, supposing this to be physically possible. We can of course agree that a woman has a right to control what happens inside her body, *so long* as what happens there isn't morally wrong – but that is just the question at issue. The question precisely is whether, if what is inside her is another human life, this imposes limits on her right to control what happens there. Nor do we want to be committed to prohibiting abortion in all cases simply because the foetus is currently living outside the mother's body. If medical science could remove a fertilised egg at conception and sustain it in life outside the womb, and did this as a matter of medical routine, we would not want to conclude that all abortions we now take to be acceptable would then not be. It could be the same blob of cells outside as inside, and the blob may be severely impaired no matter where it is located. So being inside a womb can't itself be the morally decisive factor.

The question must then be when, if ever, it is permissible to take a foetus's life, irrespective of where the foetus is situated. Is one-week termination acceptable? Is three-month? What about nine-month? Or six-year? We thus get many different questions, depending upon the stage of human development we are considering, not a simple all-or-nothing question; and we may well give different answers depending on the stage in question. What sorts of guidelines and principles should inform our answers to these questions? What features of the growing foetus should be regarded as morally relevant when considering the abortion option?

The basic difficulty here is that we have a complex gradation from something very close to contraception to something very close to infanticide. If you focus on the very earliest stages of pregnancy, you are dealing with a just-fertilised egg, when the genes of both parents are starting to mix; moments earlier you had the lucky sperm chugging in the direction of the egg and about to make physical contact. At this stage, preventing further cell development looks a lot like contraception and very unlike the killing of a grown person. But if you travel further down the temporal line, as the foetus is taking human shape – say, as far as the eighth month – you would be killing an organism disturbingly similar to a mature human. There is no sharp dividing line between this late stage of embryo development and the stages that take place once the baby has made its exit into the outside world. Hence the suspicion of infanticide in cases of late abortion.

Now some people tend to see all abortion as just so much contraception and hence feel no qualms; while others see it as all just like infanticide and thus feel an insurmountable problem. In fact both points of view contain elements of truth, depending on the stage you have in mind. The real question is how to balance these two extremes, not exaggerating either, so as to give an accurate assessment of the moral situation. *How* similar is six-week abortion (say) to contraception, at one extreme, and to infanticide, at the other? Can it be assimilated to either?

Before I try to answer this, I should say something about the standard slogans used to debate the issue, and note their inadequacies. One side, in favour of abortion rights, proclaims itself 'pro-choice'; the other side, against abortion, describes itself as 'pro-life'. The purpose of these self-selected labels is clear enough. The pro-choice group wants you to think, 'Yes, choice is generally a good thing; people should have the right to choose how to run their lives, including whether to have a child or not – it is a question of personal freedom.' The pro-life group wants you to think, instead, 'No, it is wrong to take an innocent human life; people shouldn't be allowed to erase life at will – that is murder.' Thus the issue becomes: do you believe in choice or in life?

The trouble with these labels and the dilemma they present is that they avoid the real questions; they simply don't face up to the issue. Of course, choice is a good thing, freedom is a positive value – no one doubts that, in the abstract. But not the freedom *to do wrong*, not the choice of evil or harmful acts. Imagine a political lobby in favour of legalising random murder

by any weapon you could lay your hands on. They might adver-
tise themselves as 'pro-choice', invoking the rhetoric of freedom
in their support. You couldn't fault them for upholding the
value of freedom, but you would obviously be right to object
that what they are advocating is the freedom to do wrong.
Similarly, anti-abortionists think it is morally wrong to kill a
foetus; you make no impression on their case, or on them, by
upholding the freedom to perpetrate this wrong. The 'pro-
choice' rhetoric has got the moral issue the wrong way round:
things are not morally right simply because doing them involves
choice; rather, choices are right or wrong because of the right-
ness or wrongness of the thing chosen. Insisting on the freedom
to choose whether to have a child simply begs the question
against the other side, since they take this to be tantamount to
having the right to do evil.

The 'pro-life' slogan is equally question-begging. Everyone
is pro-life in the sense that they think wilful murder is wrong;
nobody is 'anti-life'. The whole question, however, is whether
the life of a *foetus* has a certain kind of moral weight, sufficient
to overturn such considerations as that its birth may kill the
mother, or that it is mentally and physically impaired. Is its life
really on a par with the life of a ten-year-old child? The mere
word 'life' gives us no useful guidance here. Sperms and eggs
are made of living tissue, after all, so why isn't contraception
prohibited by the 'pro-life' position? Cabbages are alive too, as
are bacteria. What has to be explained is why a particular *kind*
of life, that of a foetus at a certain stage of development, has
the sort of overriding value that anti-abortionists claim. And it
is no use here to appeal to some entirely general notion of 'life'.

At this point some imaginary cases will help to soften up the
kind of absolutism that so often bedevils this debate, and enable
us to reach a balanced compromise position. Imagine that
human conception works as follows: the female becomes spon-
taneously pregnant every month without any outside help from
the male, so that a baby will be produced in nine months unless
something is done to stop it. This just happens to be the way
biology has decided to propagate the species. However, biology
has also provided an easy way out of these automatic monthly

pregnancies: if something is gently inserted in the vagina, say a finger or a penis, the pregnancy is thereby terminated. Thus sexual intercourse has exactly the opposite effect in this imaginary case from what it actually has: it cancels conception rather than causes it. Now it is clear that, unless such insertion is regularly carried out, there will soon be an awful lot of children about – enormous families, massive population explosion, possibly widespread starvation. Not a good situation at all. Suppose we came across a humanoid species in which these were the biological facts and in which monthly abortion was routinely practised in the way described. How morally bad would we think them to be? I suggest that, all things considered, we wouldn't consider them to be bad at all, assuming that they didn't leave the insertion operation until too far along in the pregnancy. We would tend to think of this kind of early natural termination as close to contraception as we practise it.

Or again, suppose that pregnancy worked thus: the mother's egg sits in a chemical environment inside her which will, after a certain amount of time, automatically trigger the egg to migrate to another part of her body in which gestation will start to occur (without any contribution from the male of the species). This migration will, however, only happen if she pulls her left ear lobe at the right time; otherwise the egg will dissolve, to be replaced with a new one six months hence. So she has to decide, on a certain day, whether to let the egg migrate: should she pull her ear lobe or not? She decides not to, because she doesn't want a baby at that time, knowing that the natural process of migration will then not occur. So not pulling her ear lobe is a kind of abortion in this imaginary case; or equally, we could say, it is a kind of contraception. It falls into neither category at all clearly. Perhaps the egg is already starting to divide before the migration occurs, so that preventing it migrating by not pulling the ear lobe has the very same kind of effect as directly terminating the existence of the clump of cells once they have migrated. Surely in this case too we would not think of refraining from pulling the ear lobe as morally equivalent to shooting someone in the head. It is much more like donning a condom.

These examples suggest that there can be no absolute prohibition on abortion under all imaginable circumstances, even where the baby will be healthy and the mother not medically threatened. The conclusion we seem to be coming to is that very early abortion resembles contraception, from a biological and moral point of view; while very late abortion is scarcely distinguishable from infanticide. What change in the blob of cells we call the foetus corresponds to this shift in moral status? When does the blob cease to be a blob and become an appropriate object of moral concern? When does a collection of human cells acquire the right not to be terminated? And in virtue of what?

We have already decided that the cut-off point can't be when the baby is ejected from the womb, i.e. is born. From the perspective of the baby's intrinsic nature, it is arbitrary at what point it steps boldly forth. Where the baby happens to be ensconced is not the crucial thing.

Some thinkers say that the foetus needs to be a *person*: that is what gives it the right to life. I think this is on the right lines, broadly speaking, but it is unsatisfactory as it stands. First, we need to distinguish between being a person and being human, since the foetus is a 'human being' virtually from the moment of conception: it is human (not reptile), and it is a being (something that exists) – so, sure, it is a human being. So what *is* meant by 'person' when it is said that a two-day-old foetus isn't yet a person? This is not terribly clear. Is a new-born infant a person? What about a severely retarded individual? Or a Martian? Do you need to have a personality? Actually or potentially? Can you stop being a person and continue to exist?

It will help to go back to our previous chapter about animals. We can ask about abortion for animals too, of course. Is it right to abort the unborn children of chimpanzees, say, given that we agree that it is wrong to murder adult chimpanzees? Well, the person test looks pretty unhelpful here: is a chimpanzee a person? That sounds odd because we don't tend to use the word 'person' of animals. But if the chimpanzee isn't a person its offspring aren't either. So if we want to extend our view of the rights and wrongs of human abortion to abortion in other species, as I think we should, then we need another way of describing the case. If the late abortion of unborn chimps is as wrong as chimp infanticide, this can hardly be because the chimp foetus acquires the status of personhood. It must be because of something else it has that it didn't have earlier on. Persons may have this, but it can be possessed by non-persons too. What then is the magic ingredient? I hope that what I am about to suggest has become pretty obvious to the reader by now. What makes a foetus morally valuable is basically what makes an animal morally valuable: *sentience*. When the foetal organism, of whatever species, has become complex enough, by the division of cells and so forth, to have feeling and perception – consciousness – that is the time at which its rights kick in. Awareness is what makes the difference, having an inner mental life. Some animal organisms lack sentience, like the amoeba or the bacterium, so they do not warrant the same treatment as organisms rich in sentience, like dogs or cats or monkeys. And the closer an embryo is to this insentient condition, no matter what its species, the less moral weight it has. The greater its sentience the more we have to take its interests into account. So foetal rights turn on essentially the same thing as animal rights. The dividing-line is drawn similarly in the two cases. Conscious life is the key consideration.

This criterion is not, of course, absolutely precise (nor uncontroversial!), since sentience comes in many forms and is not easy to detect in all its manifestations. But it is less arbitrary than the others we have canvassed and it fits well with our general moral intuitions about right and wrong. Importantly, it unifies the abortion issue with the considerations that bear on our treatment of animals, thus conferring a nice simplicity on our moral principles.

The sentience criterion also has the advantage of coming in degrees: organisms can be more or less rich in sentience, depending on how complex their mental life is. A human foetus will gradually acquire more sentience as its nervous system develops and it experiences more things as pleasant or painful. This implies that the longer the foetus has to develop the more serious is the act of aborting it, so that in the final stages it will be as serious as post-natal infanticide. We thus have an explanation of the wrongness of late abortion that fits the fact that it

gets more wrong the longer you wait. Accordingly, the longer
you wait the better reason you need to make the abortion
morally defensible: that is, the harder it becomes to override the
value attaching to the foetus's life. The wrongness comes in
degrees because sentience comes in degrees. When you wrongly
take a life, what you are taking is a centre of consciousness. But
where there is no such centre, the question of wrongness does
not arise.

This more-or-less position will not suit those who like their
morality black and white; nor will it please people who want
moral principles to be so absolute as not to allow exceptions in
the face of overriding reasons. The issue of abortion seems to
me to show that a sensible morality cannot be like that. Too
many things have to be taken into account. The sentience
criterion offers, I think, the most reasonable and realistic approach to the question of abortion, in which no simple
all-or-nothing rules are going to be forthcoming. It is a matter
of balance and judgement, guided by the idea that sentience is
a central source of value. You can't just invoke some simple
general principle – like 'choice' or 'the right to life' – and hope
to crank out a straightforward answer applicable to all cases.
Abortion is not 'always wrong', but nor is it 'always permissible'.
It depends on the details of the case – both the state of the
foetus and the consequences of giving birth to it for all concerned. What I am suggesting is that in assessing these details
the underlying concern, so far as the welfare of the foetus is
concerned, is its degree of sentience. Not its *potential* degree of
sentience, mark you, since even the unjoined sperm and egg
have potential sentience – if you let them join they will produce
a fully sentient human adult. No, its actual degree of sentience
– a mental interior, an inner light.

On this way of looking at the matter, the wrongness of killing
a foetus at a certain stage of development goes with the wrongness of acting on it in ways that stop short of killing it. Should
we be allowed to use human foetuses for scientific experiments
– say, experiments that may benefit children in the future? This
question can be raised either about the foetus inside the mother
or about the foetus *sans* mother, produced (say) by genetic

engineering. This is quite a hard question, but the answer to it suggested by our previous discussion is that such experiments are permissible only if there is no pain involved for the foetus – indeed only if it has not yet reached the condition of sentience at all. Suppose a mother wants an abortion for some sufficiently good reason: can her doctor legitimately ask her to let the foetus be experimented on while it is still alive inside her, with the hope of finding a cure for some terrible disease? Well, putting aside for now general questions about using one being as a means to benefit others, the answer should depend upon the level of sentience reached by the foetus. Roughly, it should be allowed only if the degree of sentience is vanishingly low or entirely absent (and depending also, of course, on how beneficial to others the experiment is likely to be).

The question of abortion is not very pleasant to write or think about. Endorsing killing always goes against the grain, or should do, and the decision to abort is full of hard choices. People tend to get very worked up on the subject, one way or the other. But it is essential to think carefully about the question and to keep a cool head while doing so. Vague slogans and political posturing are not the way to handle the issue. Nor will it do to pretend that no conflicts of interest arise here. Abortion, clearly, is a serious matter, not to be undertaken lightly. It is certainly no substitute for contraception. It is, I have suggested, morally acceptable to abort early, but very strong reason is needed to justify late abortion.

4

Violence

Violence may be defined as doing harm to a sentient being on purpose. Car accidents don't involve violence, by this definition, since they are not (usually) intended to cause the harm they do; similarly for surgery that goes awry or the barber's nick. Violence, as I mean to discuss it here, involves deliberately causing damage or pain or death to someone else, a person or an animal. And the main question for discussion is whether violence in this sense can ever be justified. Is it ever right, or at least not wrong, to harm others intentionally? And if so, under what conditions? When, if ever, is violence morally excusable?

What kinds of acts fall under this general heading? Most obviously, acts that involve damage to the body: bruises, wounds, broken bones, mutilation, as well as the traceless pain of the skilled torturer. So punching or shooting someone might be taken as paradigms of the violent act. Boxing, warfare and wife-battering are all clear cases of this sort of physical violence. But this is not the only kind of act that causes harm to others, because physical harm is not the only kind of harm there is: there is also emotional or psychological harm. No discussion of the ethics of violence would be complete without mentioning this important category of intentional harm. Emotional harm may often be caused by physical violence, as with the emotional trauma that often accompanies (say) a violent mugging or the physical abuse of a child; but it can also be caused purely verbally, and even by gesture.

The central cases are insult, slander, belittlement, harping on painful subjects. This kind of verbal violence frequently goes with anger and shouting, often directed at someone not in a position to answer back. The aim is to hurt the other person emotionally, to cause them mental pain and anguish. This can substitute for, or supplement, the causing of physical pain by bodily means. It can, indeed, be worse in its effects than passing physical violence. Thus bullies can come in different varieties: from the plain physical bully of the playground to the intellectual bully of the academic seminar room – not to speak of the double-barrelled kind personified by the aggressive domineering father. Violence is not merely a matter of the fists and the gun; it can be perpetrated also through words and looks. Nor should it be made light of simply because the wounds inflicted are not visible on the victim's body. There are wounds we carry around inside, which can take far longer to heal than a simple black eye. Your body will not automatically cure you of emotional pain.

We can divide violent acts, whether physical or mental, into two categories, according to whether the harm is meant as a means or as an end. When it is meant as an end the aggressor simply wants to cause pain and damage to the other person, but not as a way of achieving something else he or she wants. This may come from the revenge motive, or it may be pure sadism, or it may issue from some quirk in the aggressor's psychological make-up – as with the warped serial killer. It is violence for its own sake. The use of violence as a means to some further end, where the end may not in itself essentially involve violence, is another matter. Thus, a parent may spank a child in order to stop her from stealing apples, or a tyrant may kill and torture his subjects in order to prevent them from rebelling. This use of violence is incidental in that the aggressor might well be happy to use some other means if that sufficed to bring about the desired effect; it is just that violence is often a remarkably efficient way of getting people to do what they don't want to do. Violence, and the fear of it, are thus often used as a means of control – either codified in the law of the land or part of the unwritten 'law of the jungle'. Both governments and gangs use violence, each in their own way, to enforce control over people.

These two categories of violence need to be kept distinct because they raise rather different ethical issues. Plainly, if violence is ever to be justified, it is far more likely that it will be violence as a means that will be justifiable, not violence as an end in itself. You may believe that revenge justifies violence, but this is a different kind of issue from that of (say) the resort to violence in self-defence. The question I am most concerned with here is the use of violence as a means – either to some definite further objective or as a general deterrent against future violence. So: when may you use violence as a means to secure an end you desire?

This question is forced upon us because of the relationship, or lack of it, between power and justice in human affairs. I am sorry to have to report that people don't always do as they ought. They often act unjustly, wickedly, reprehensibly. They steal, rape, murder, torture, threaten. Whole countries steal other countries, murdering their citizens, reducing them to subservience and poverty. And individuals do some terrible things to each other, on the street, in the home. You just have to read the newspapers! Goodness and justice don't always rule human conduct. Some people are really very nasty, or at least do some very nasty things. When such people can't get what they want by legitimate means they often resort to force: they violently take what they cannot obtain by rational persuasion or natural right.

Now it is easy to see that such a use of force cannot be justified, since it is by definition unjust and immoral. It shoulders justice aside and proceeds by other means. The harder question concerns the use of force and violence to *rectify* injustice – that is, the use of force and violence *on the side* of justice. When does justice license the use of violence to achieve its legitimate ends? When is it right to promote the moral good by intentionally harming others? When does right justify might?

It is natural to feel, in a first flush of innocence, that it is never right to use violence, no matter how just the cause, since violence is in itself a bad and evil thing. This view is sometimes called 'pacifism', especially in relation to the violence of war. It counsels always meeting violence with non-violence. Is pacifism defensible? Violence, of course, as the pacifist insists, is in itself a bad thing; but the question is whether this intrinsic badness can ever be overridden by a greater good. And it seems to me quite clear that absolute pacifism is really not a tenable moral position, at least as an exceptionless principle prohibiting violence in any circumstances – though it may be sensible and right in more cases than people tend to allow. Any number of hackneyed examples show that it is too extreme and could lead to very unfortunate results.

Thus suppose your crazed next-door neighbour bursts into your house one night, drunk and wielding a shotgun, and announces his intention of shooting your entire family because he doesn't like the colour you have painted your house. You choose not to believe him, despite the fact that another family in the neighbourhood was recently massacred by shotgun and the killer not yet caught. You ask him please to put the gun down. He responds by shooting your grandmother and then turns the gun in the direction of your ten-year-old son. What should you do? As it happens, there is a loose rafter in the ceiling and you know that if you cough loudly it will fall down and hit the killer on the head, knocking him out, maybe even killing him. Clearly, I say, you should cough. And if you think that you might not be *sure* he'll kill anyone else, then imagine him with a knife and already stabbing a member of your family with it.

I think we should all want to say that in this kind of case it is legitimate and proper to use violence to defend yourself and others from the violence of the bad guy. It may be regrettable, you may feel bad afterwards – but it isn't morally wrong. Equally, if one state violently invades another state for no other reason than its own enrichment, you are morally entitled as a citizen of the invaded state to protect it from aggression. In sum, then, aggression may be met with aggression as a means of self-defence. So the extreme pacifist view is unacceptable.

There is an opposite viewpoint to that of pacifism that has no convenient label, which I will call 'machoism' for what should become obvious reasons. It is a very common view and is not widely deplored. The essence of it is that it is sometimes acceptable to meet non-violence with violence. You can hit out even though no one is trying to hit you or anyone else. Thus in many a macho movie we see various kinds of verbal insult met with a punch or worse. This is deemed okay, even admirable, where the insult is aimed at something we hold particularly dear or sacred. These sacred things vary, but the following are typical: race, religion, country, mother, potency. If someone insults you by deriding any of these things, by name-calling or some other verbal slur, it is deemed acceptable to deck him, break his jaw, do him some physical damage. It is thought to be 'unmanly' not to respond with violence to insults against what we hold sacred; perhaps not the extreme of violence, but some show of physical aggression. This is essentially the idea that we can meet certain acts of real or attempted emotional violence with straight physical violence. For who would not raise his fists to defend his mother's honour against an evil slur? Who would be so cowardly as to let a racial insult go by unpunished? Call me that again and I'll slug you!

It seems to me that this machoist view is quite wrong, morally speaking. It is wrong as a matter of principle and it is the source of large amounts of avoidable violence. The reason it is wrong in principle is enshrined in an old motto which is often taken to promote violence but in fact has an opposite tendency: 'an eye for an eye and a tooth for a tooth.' The key point about this motto, as originally intended, is that it prohibits exacting an eye for a tooth – only a *tooth* may be taken for a tooth. It insists, that is, on replying in kind to an injury, not stepping up the response with something of a different order. So in the case of insult the motto tells us to reply with an insult or some equivalent verbal performance, but *not* with a blow to the head. The verbal response might be an expression of contempt or a hoot of derisive laughter, or it might be something comparably insulting; it might even be a stony stare. The time to reply with a blow is when a blow is aimed at you (or someone else), not when a word is.

This principle commends itself on the score of natural justice, but it also contains a sensible piece of practical wisdom. One of the most dangerous aspects of violence is its tendency to spiral and magnify – to 'escalate' as they say. If someone else steps up the violence, then you feel that you are entitled to step it up a notch too; and so in a way you are, since to reply in kind would *be* to step up the violence some more again – once the other person has already stepped it up. So the rule should be: never step it up to start with. That way the other guy has no reason to step it up in turn, and hence you have no reason to go one step further than him. This point applies to all sorts of violence, emotional as well as physical, verbal and bodily. If someone insults you relatively mildly for some reason, you should insult them mildly back, according to our motto, not insult them extremely. That is only just and fair. A terrific amount of strife and harm is caused in human relationships by not observing this simple principle. Remember, once you step up the violence the other person can step it up to the same level and also by as much as you originally stepped it up – and still claim not to be violating the principle of equal response. Don't give them that excuse! Once this process is under way you can find yourself moving by predictable steps from a mild insult at first to acts of murder in the end. If A decides to take an eye for a tooth, B will want A's head for that eye – precisely because A went beyond what was fair, so inviting a response in kind.

What goes for verbal insult also goes for things like spitting, though here the temptation to slug in response may be very great. If someone spits at you, or on you, as a gesture of disrespect, the right response is not to punch them on the nose, since this is to move to a higher order of violence. The right response is to spit back, or perhaps avail yourself of the nearest piece of dog-do; if not then, later. It may be 'human' to lash out at someone who spits at you, but I don't think it is morally right.

You will notice that the principle of equal response, inter-preted as setting a limit on what can be done to an aggressor, needn't be taken to prescribe *always* replying equally. It simply says you shouldn't go beyond this and it is legitimate to go as far as this. But there may well be cases in which there is no need to go that far to achieve your good ends. An attempt to kill needn't be met with killing; it may be met with something less drastic, if that will be enough to eliminate the threat. Mercy often consists in not doing what you could do morally – not exacting the pound of flesh. Defensive violence has an instrumental justification – to prevent harm to yourself and others – and if something lesser will do, a merciful person will be satisfied with that. It will depend on the details of the case.

So far we have focused on defence of the person against violence, and adopted the common view that violence in return is justified in such cases, subject to certain guidelines. But matters are not quite so simple, since not all violence occurs, so to speak, in the present. We can all see that if someone is currently attacking you or your child you are entitled to protect yourself or her. But what about the case in which there is a credible future threat to yourself or your child – either preceded by earlier violence or merely by the promise of it? The standard case here is that of the battered wife whose husband threatens to beat her again in the future. Can she take violent steps today to prevent this happening tomorrow? I think in principle she can, so long as she has good reason to be afraid, and she does only what is necessary to protect herself in the future – or gets someone else to do it. It is not enough rather to suspect that someone *might* do you damage, though they haven't ever done it in the past; you have to be *sure* they will – or else you will be guilty of unjustified violence yourself. Pre-emptive violence is a tricky matter and should be carried out only when the threat is real and pressing, not 'just in case' something is done to you.

This applies not only to physical violence but also to the kind of emotional violence involved (say) in taking someone to court to settle a personal dispute that could be settled without taking this step. You shouldn't do this just on the off-chance that the other party might do the same to you. Resorting to lawyers in personal matters can be an act of violence in its own way, and is often so intended. Like other forms of force, it should be resorted to only when absolutely necessary. In matters of divorce, for example, much trouble is caused by one party rushing to lawyers just in the case the other does, and extracting as much as he or she legally can on the hypothesis that the other person will do the same. But the mere *possibility* that someone may try to do you harm is not a good reason for *actually* harming them first. You have to be certain.

There is a further aspect of the motto, as it is commonly understood, that needs to be addressed. So far I have taken it in a broadly defensive way, as a principle about violent defence against unjust violence, present or looming. This includes direct attack, credible threat of future attack, and even enforced social suppression, as with certain forms of political tyranny. But the motto has often been taken to imply something wider about reactive violence, and we have to ask whether this wider principle is morally acceptable. I mean the idea that an injury, physical or mental, can be justifiably met with another injury even when this return injury has no defensive intention or effect. You can take someone else's tooth, not only to protect your tooth, but also because that person *has* taken your tooth. This is the idea of revenge, which is connected to the idea of 'moral balance' – the bad guy should suffer in proportion to the suffering he has caused. Here we enter murky and perilous waters, in which it is not easy to retain clear vision. The revenge motive is certainly a deep and persistent human trait, stemming from the feeling that the aggressor should not be allowed to 'get away with it'. He must *pay*. Punishment is his due, and it is our duty to extract it. Thus we cheer when the evil-doer comes to a sticky end, especially when he is hoist with his own petard. Revenge, they say, is sweet – and this sweetness has nothing to do, intrinsically, with self-defence. But is it right?

It is not at all clear what positive good is done by acts of revenge. Whom do they benefit? Such acts may, of course, have a deterrent effect and thus prevent further wrongdoing in the future; people will see that they can't get away with violence scot-free, and will be less ready to perpetrate it. This is a legitimate enough reason to repay violence with violence, assuming the deterrence works: the bully should be bullied in return, so that he and other bullies will be deterred from their bullying – if that is indeed the likely result. But considered independently of deterrence, which anyway is not what revenge is usually all about, revenge seems merely to add to the amount of violence in the world, rather than to diminish it – which is what the point of violence in a just cause is supposed to be. It looks a lot like gratuitous violence, violence that does not seek a peaceful end. It is violence that stops with itself, which is its own point. An act of revenge adds one more violent episode to the world without any expectation of decreasing violence in the long run. Its justification is the violence that has occurred in the past, not the reduction of violence in the future.

My own feeling is that I would find it hard to carry out such purely vengeful violence, no matter how loathsome the original act was, since no further good would be served by it; but I have to admit that I find it satisfying when it happens by nature, as it were. I am grimly glad that Hitler perished as he did, but I would be reluctant to pull the trigger on him *simply* as revenge for his terrible crimes – and not, say, to prevent further crimes by him or others of like mind. It is as if I feel that nature should take revenge for us, but we should eschew it, since it is uncomfortably similar to that for which it is done – violence for the sake of no greater good. It makes harm an end in itself. The revenge motive regards violence itself as a desirable object. I therefore think the eye-for-an-eye motto should not encourage us to seek revenge, but should only tell us by what means we can defend ourselves against unwarranted violence.

Some of my gentler readers may feel that I am being a little too ready to return violence with violence. Shouldn't other avenues be explored first? Doesn't violence invariably lead to more violence? Shouldn't we give peace a chance? These are entirely sensible queries and the sentiments they express have my full support. Violence is indeed horrible and must only be used as a last resort, and one adopted with a heavy heart, not with jubilation. But the sad fact is that there are people in this world who, for one reason or another, understand and respond to nothing else. They are blind to justice and decency, and are even openly contemptuous of these values; they are simply not moved by rational moral persuasion. Violence, for them, is a way of life – the best way they know for getting what they want. We see this as much in our daily and family lives as we do on the level of street crime and international politics. Sometimes, then, there is just no other way to prevent violent miscreants causing great harm. By all means, try peaceful methods first, but be ready for the person who will not listen. As a piece of practical advice, then, I would say, yes, don't rush to return violence with violence, try reason first, since the aggressor *may* feel that justice is on his side and yet be persuaded out of this belief, so ceasing his violence. But once this is shown to be hopeless be ready to cause him harm in order to prevent further harm to yourself and others, since he will *only* be moved by harm to himself. It is terrible, I know, but there are times when it has to be.

So far war and personal assault have been our primary focus, but there are a number of other areas in which the morality of violence needs to be examined; I will briefly consider suicide, violent sports and the corporal punishment of children.

Suicide is violence against oneself: killing someone who happens to be identical with the killer. Is this morally wrong? It is certainly not, save in exceptional cases, justified by previous or impending violence on the part of the person who is to be killed. People don't usually kill themselves for defensive reasons! So it may seem to follow from our previous principles that suicide must be immoral, since it entails violence against someone who has committed no violence – or none that is being reciprocated in the act of suicide. A compulsive killer might decide that it would be best for his future victims if he did away with himself, but this is not the usual case.

However, this would be a crude and unconvincing use of our earlier principles. Suicide must be made an exception to the rules applying to violence against *others*. The reason for this is just that there are many things that it is not immoral to do to oneself voluntarily but that it would be immoral to do to others against their will. I have a perfect right to make myself do thirty press-ups despite the pain it causes me, but it would be mean and wrong for me to make you do this if you didn't want to. I can give myself a tattoo, but I shouldn't compel you to have one. I can eat unhealthy food, but I shouldn't force it down your throat. That is, I have rights over my own person that I don't have over your person, and one of these is the right to end my life if I see fit. Or rather, nothing in what we have said so far about violence implies that suicide is morally wrong. It may not be sensible or wise of me, but it isn't immoral of me in the way that my murdering you would be immoral. Violence to oneself isn't like unwarranted aggression against others, since one has special rights over one's own person.

The case of suicide is thus clearly an exception to our general rule, but violent sports are not so clearly exempt. This is because the violence done there *is* violence to another person. Take boxing: here two people knock each other about in a way that you or I wouldn't care for. Real violence is definitely being done by one person to another. It is not like punching yourself, something that you have a right to do. Much the same is true of other 'contact sports'. So is boxing immoral? Are the two boxers inflicting unjustifiable violence on each other? Forget the fact that boxing is a public spectacle in which a lot of dubious money is made; just suppose that two men agree to slug it out between them in private to see who is the better slugger. The point about this, which makes it different from ordinary assault, is that both participants engage in the violence voluntarily. One fighter agrees with the other that they will hit each other; this is a kind of contract between them. Yes, there is intentional harm, and its purpose is not to prevent further violence: but the participants have knowingly consented to perpetrate this mutual harm. Thus violent sports differ crucially from ordinary criminal aggression, precisely because they are entered into voluntarily. It may well be that such agreements should not be allowed, say because they promote violence in society at large or because poverty will drive some people into these dangerous pursuits. But the fact that they involve voluntary contracts sets them apart from other types of violence, which are anything but voluntary. Thus our earlier considerations do not entail that boxing is immoral and should be banned. Maybe it should be, but not for the same reason that prohibits other forms of violence.

What about hitting children then? Is this too an exception? It is widely assumed that parents do have the right to inflict violence on their children, for a variety of reasons. These include disobedience, naughtiness and disrespect, as well as to educate them against danger. None of these has anything to do with self-defence against the violence of children. In some cases these punishments can be quite extreme, like being soundly thrashed for holding your fork in the wrong hand; in others it may be a simple slap on the cheek for stealing money from your mother's purse. I myself would say that all such acts of violence are to be condemned. Consistency requires it. Since these are not cases of self-defence of the parent against the child, or even acts of revenge for the child's earlier violence, they are really no different, morally, from hitting another adult because he disobeys you or does something you think is wrong. Only violence can justify violence, and in the vast majority of cases parental violence against children has no such justification. Naughtiness and disobedience are simply not forms of violence. We can all see this when it comes to other adults, but we inconsistently take a different view where children are concerned. I don't think I can hit my adult brother because he always leaves his muddy shoes on the carpet, but there are plenty of people who think nothing of doing this to their children. Why? There is no moral justification for it. Violence against children should be regarded like any other kind of violence: immoral unless prompted by the child's own aggression, and subject to the same limitations. Hitting children is wrong in the same way hitting adults is. Indeed since children often don't know what they are doing and are pretty harmless anyway, it is even *less* reasonable to visit reciprocal violence on them.

This point applies as much to verbal violence as to physical violence. Shouting at children, hurting their feelings, verbally abusing them – these are all cases of wrongful emotional aggression. And since an awful lot of this goes on within families, I would say that there is far too much violence against children. Parents should stop doing it, *now*. The rules that govern violence in the adult world should be extended to children.

This touches on the question of why people so often resort to violence when they have no justification for doing do. It could be that as children they were themselves so often the victims of acts of violence that had no sound moral justification. They were constantly being hit or shouted at when they had themselves not done either of these things. Thus children grow up accustomed to the idea that violence is an acceptable response to intrinsically non-violent (though possibly bad) acts. This conditions people into accepting forms of violence in the world that have no moral basis, since this was the daily state of affairs at home. If we are serious about trying to reduce the amount of violence in the world, I think we should begin with the family: children should be accorded the same respect and protection from violence as anyone else. They shouldn't grow up with the idea that you are allowed to harm people who haven't harmed you.

5

Sex

Human beings come with a range of needs and desires, impulses and feelings. These centre round certain specific sorts of activity: eating, playing, working, having sex. Because of our mental and biological make-up we like to engage in these activities, and we are apt to find not engaging in them (for any length of time) frustrating and depressing. We take these things to be integral to our happiness and well-being, to be a large part of what gives human life its point. In the case of sex, the need is often spoken of as a *drive*, as if it forces itself on our will from outside. We talk of being starved of sex and in other less polite ways of the state of sexual deprivation. Unlike eating, which you have to do in order to stay alive, we don't need sex literally to keep going; but we do – at least most of us – need sex in order to find life fulfilling. The enormous place occupied by sex in human life is amply attested by its role in art, both classical and popular, as well as in advertising and ordinary conversation – not to mention its private place in our own heated imagination. Among the facts of life, sex is one of the biggest. What moral rules should be applied to sexual behaviour? When sex meets ethics what should we, as both sexual and ethical beings, do about it?

I said in the first chapter that a basic moral axiom is that people should have the freedom to do what they want to do so long as this doesn't interfere with other people's freedom to do what *they* want. I should be able to do what I like with my life, so long as this doesn't stop other people doing what they like with theirs. It is wrong to deprive people of their freedom for no good reason, since their happiness largely resides in the extent of their freedom. We should be tolerant of others, up to the point at which their actions infringe our own liberty.

How does this simple point of view apply to the case of sexual freedom? The answer comes easily: people should be allowed to exercise their sexual freedom, to engage in the sexual activities of their choice, so long as this doesn't harm or confine or thwart others. Sex should be treated rather like eating: people should be allowed to eat what they like when they like, so long as this doesn't mess up other people's (and animals') lives. It is wrong to prevent people eating what they want to eat, if this does no harm to anyone else. Cannibalism is of course immoral because it does interfere with others, but there can be no *moral* objection to eating boiled cabbage or baked beans or chip sandwiches. Comparably, then, it is wrong to have sex with people who don't want to have it with you, or don't want to have it in the way you do, but it is not wrong to have it with someone who shares your desire. Rape is wrong, but voluntary intercourse is fine. This follows from the general principle that freedom is a supreme good that requires a certain special kind of reason to curtail. Viewed in this way then, it appears that sexual ethics can be summed up very simply: complete sexual tolerance, guided only by the principle of non-interference with others. You can do whatever you like, provided you don't get in anyone else's way. So long as there is mutual consent, the sky is the limit.

Can we therefore conclude this chapter right here and move on to morally juicier subjects? No, because there are various kinds of objection to the pleasingly simple position just outlined. Things are not quite so straightforward. Some of these objections, familiar enough to most of us, will turn out to lack rational foundation, but others call for greater subtlety in our conception of sexual rectitude. The basic principle is sound enough for most purposes, but it needs to be qualified in certain respects. I will divide my discussion into two parts: in the first part, I will talk about certain restrictions on sexual freedom that don't turn on the *normality* of the kind of sexual activity at issue, in the second with the question of sexual perversion or abnormality, to see whether any reasonable restrictions emerge from this concept. First, should there be any restrictions on 'normal' sex? Secondly, should 'abnormal' sex be restricted?

The first set of possible restrictions concerns the relations between (a) sex and love, (b) sex and marriage, and (c) sex and disease. In each case we have to ask whether the second item in each of these pairs imposes reasonable moral limits on sexual activity. Let us start with love.

Love and sexual desire frequently go together, but they are not the same thing. You can want to have sex with someone you don't love, and you can love someone you don't want to have sex with. Our concern here is with the first of these – sex without love. There is a strain of moral thinking that wishes to put a stop to that kind of thing, that says sex is wrong unless backed by love.

This is surely too tight a restraint to place on sexual activity; nor does it have any clear moral basis. To take an extreme possibility, suppose that human beings were biologically incapable of love – they just didn't have it in them (most species of animal are presumably like this). Would that mean that it is always morally wrong for humans to have sex with each other? Why? If they accepted the moral prohibition against loveless sex, they would (a) die out as a species and (b) have much less enjoyable lives. That can't be right, can it?

Less drastically, what about those periods, sometimes distressingly long, during which you have no one to love and yet still have sexual desires? Why should you be made to suffer, not just the state of lovelessness but also the state of chronic sexual frustration? In fact if people feel that sex must always be sanctified by love, they will tend to persuade themselves that they are in love precisely in order to justify having sex to themselves. This will lead to emotional dishonesty and many unhappy love affairs. Doubtless sex has a special quality when love enters into it, but that shouldn't mean that the other kind of sex must be felt as a burden to the conscience. Perhaps too there is something amiss with a person who finds sex and love mutually incompatible, but again this doesn't imply that loveless sex is morally wrong. It should be voluntary for both parties, yes, and there should be no deception involved, and perhaps the possibility of love should not be wholly excluded – but it is too much to require people always to be in love with their sexual partners. Respect, consideration, even affection – but love is a lot to ask, every time.

As for sex and marriage, we all know that it used to be held, with some rigidity, that sex before, or outside, marriage is morally wrong. So people would approach their wedding night in a state of profound sexual ignorance – with no practical know-how at all. Nowadays few people take this ban very seriously, regarding it as really just a roundabout way of avoiding 'illegitimate' children, now superseded by generally available contraception. I am with the spirit of the times on this question: there is no good reason for thinking that acts of intercourse before the marriage ceremony are wicked or shameful, while those that immediately follow are blessed. The marriage ceremony isn't a kind of moral magic, capable of transforming the bad to the good just like that. Insisting on this precondition for sex will only trap people into unsuitable marriages, simply because they are keen – too keen! – to begin their sexual lives. And what if you can't find a marriage partner at all?

Yet perhaps there is one thing to be said for the no-sex-before-marriage idea, or at least for what may lie behind it: the thought that having sex with someone is a sort of personal contract, an agreement carrying certain responsibilities. This contract involves not knowingly risking the transmission of disease, not betraying your partner's confidence, acting afterwards with kindness and consideration, not telling lies about your long-term intentions, and so forth. Sex shouldn't be separated from these kinds of personal commitment – from *trust*, in a word – even though the contract needn't consist in a formal marriage. In this respect, then, it isn't exactly like eating a tasty meal, since there is another *person* on the receiving end of the act. That said though, the contract can be informal and flexible, depending on the expectations and wishes of each partner; what matters is that no one pull a fast one. Monogamy for the duration, for example, is often part of what each partner expects of the other. But people should have the freedom to make the kinds of sexual contract they want and not be limited to a single kind – such as conventional marriage.

I mentioned the transmission of disease through sexual contact. This has always been a major concern in sexual ethics and is doubly urgent now that we have AIDS to contend with. Clearly it is morally wrong to have sex with someone when there is a good chance they will contract a disease from you – as wrong as strolling into a school full of kids when you are the bearer of some highly contagious and lethal infection. This is a straight case of causing harm to others in the pursuit of your own selfish interests. However, there is a deeply rooted tendency for people to misunderstand the relationship between sex and disease. Superstitiously, they believe that the link between the two somehow shows the fundamental immorality of sex; and this is particularly true for diseases that are most easily transmitted through kinds of sexual act commonly regarded as 'abnormal' – anal sex, for example. There is thus a tendency to see disease as the punishment for sex, as a proof of its sinfulness.

What we need to be clear about here are the elementary medical facts of disease transmission; then we shall see that it is really just an accident, from a moral point of view, that sex transmits disease. The diseases in question are bacterial and viral; they result from micro-organisms that live in the bloodstream and internal organs of the body. These are the same kinds of agents that cause flu or polio or malaria. They get into you and then do damage to your body, sometimes fatal damage. The little blighters hop from one body to another, using whatever method of contagion is available to them; they can't get into you by magic. The quickest and most efficient way to body-hop, from the germ's point of view, would be simply to take some blood from one person and inject it into another; but this hardly ever happens, so diseases have evolved other ways of getting around. Some travel in the air, expelled from the lungs as you breathe, but many use the obvious method of direct bodily contact, especially the kinds that enable them to get through the barrier provided by the skin. Naturally then, from a purely biological point of view, sexual contact is going to be an excellent way to get from one body to another, because of the physical intimacy involved. Hence there are bound to be diseases that specialise in this mode of transmission – as there are diseases that specialise in using air currents to get from one place to another. Consequently, there exist sexually transmitted diseases. This isn't because the disease is some kind of cosmic punishment. It is simply that sex involves bodily contact and, given the nature of disease as a biological phenomenon, micro-organisms exploit this contact to propagate themselves. They don't have any moral views about sexual morality; they are just using the most convenient way to invade another organism. If sex didn't involve any kind of contact, of the kind that micro-organisms can exploit – say, you did it over the phone – there would be no sexually transmitted diseases, no matter *how* promiscuous and irresponsible this telephonic sex was. In a sense then, it is just bad luck that sex involves the kind of personal contact that diseases rely on. If prayer entailed the kind of close bodily contact typical of sex, there would be religiously transmitted diseases – and not because there is any-thing wicked about prayer! Doctors are especially vulnerable to AIDS, given the nature of their contact with AIDS patients, but no one think this shows that doctoring is immoral. The right attitude to the link between sex and disease is to recognise it for what it really is and then take suitable precautions to prevent disease from spreading. Avoid risky sex, use a condom, get checked – but don't wax moralistic and metaphysical about this being Nature's punishment for sexual immorality. After all no one thinks that flu is divine retribution for *talking* to other people!

So far we have mainly been considering possible restrictions on so-called normal sex – ordinary heterosexual intercourse between consenting adults. I now want to talk a bit about the three Ps: perversion, prostitution and promiscuity. These are each cases in which it is often said that the sexual activity in question is abnormal or irregular in some way, a way that invites moral censure. Is there any real basis for such judgements? What, if anything, is wrong with being a P-person? Let us start with perversion, the least straightforward of the three.

People vary in what they would put on their list of perver-

sions, but the following would appear on many lists: any homosexual act, cunnilingus and fellatio, anal sex, sado-masochism,
sex with children, sex with animals, sex with furniture, dressing
up like a baby or a vicar in sexual contexts, masturbation, the
use of pornography, fornicating in airplane lavatories – and no
doubt many others. People who do these things are accordingly
labelled *perverts* and denounced for sexual immorality. Now I
don't want to talk about each of these heterogeneous items in
any detail; my aim is to work out some general principles than
can be applied, possibly with supplementation, to any alleged
case of perversion to decide whether there is really anything
morally wrong with it. (If you don't like the list above, draw up
your own.)

There are two extreme views on the perversion question,
often powered by the white heat of a particular ideology, either
'liberal' or 'conservative'. On the one hand, there is the view
that none of these activities can be justifiably criticised: people
should be allowed to do whatever they want, so long as there is
consent, and it is not our place to moralise about what they do
in private with likeminded people. (The case of child sex is likely
to be made an exception to this rule, because a child's consent
doesn't count.) It is mere prejudice, according to this view, to
label one kind of sex 'normal' and another 'abnormal', one
straight and another bent. The very concept of perversion
should be abandoned, or at least stripped of pejorative over-
tones. If someone wants to have sex only with computers, who
are we to criticise and condemn? Hey, whatever turns you on –
just go with the flow.

On the other hand, there is the view that only missionary-po-
sition heterosexual intercourse is acceptable, possibly preceded
by a bit of manual foreplay to get the ball rolling. All the rest is
'dirty', evidence of a sick mind, the work of the devil, and so
forth. If you find yourself visited with any of these deviant
impulses, you must suppress them, see a therapist, pray for
help. *Don't* go with it. Go against it. Pervert!

Which of these opposite extremes is right? I hope that at least
some of my readers feel unsure, at any rate about *which* items
on my list should be shunned or frowned upon. Certainly, *I* don't

think the matter is entirely simple and straightforward, though I have much more sympathy for the liberal view, because of its conformity to the principle of maximising individual freedom. Let us try to keep a steady head, never easy in genital controversy, and begin by asking what is meant by the word 'perversion' anyway. My dictionary says: 'to pervert: to turn aside (thing) from its proper use or nature.' Thus, you can pervert justice, you can pervert art, you can pervert sport – in each case you deflect something from its true or proper course. So, can you pervert sex – can you deflect sexual desire from its true or proper course? To make sense of this, we obviously need some concept of what the 'proper use or nature' of human sexual desire is, of what determines this. We also need to ask whether it is always morally objectionable to divert something from its 'proper use', since that seems to depend upon whether what is thus proper is also good. You can pervert a criminal organisation by deflecting its hit squad from their 'proper use', but in this case what you do is good, since the proper use of a hit squad is murder, which is bad.

From a purely biological perspective, the human sex drive has as its primary object sexual activity of a kind that would lead to conception if it occurred in the right circumstances for this to happen. Our genes programme us to have sex in order that reproduction shall occur. But of course there is more to sexual desire than this purely biological function; it also has an emotional or personal side. Sex makes us relate in certain ways to other persons *as persons*; it is connected in all sorts of respects to our nature as social beings. I would like to suggest that the proper nature of sex, from a psychological point of view, involves a desire for another person as a sentient and physical entity: it is a complex passion aimed at another person conceived as possessing a sensual nature. That sensual nature is the proper object of sexual attention – a living body capable of sexual feelings and desires. If sexual desire becomes detached from such an object, it can be said to have been perverted from its proper course.

Compare eating. Biologically, the function of eating is bodily sustenance. Psychologically, it also involves pleasure, social relationships, and an aesthetic sense. This desire can be perverted from its natural course if, say, you eat only to cure depression, thus overeating; or if certain foods are consumed solely in order to irritate your mother, irrespective of their nutritional value and tastiness.

Or consider love and friendship. Their primary object is to bring about emotionally satisfying relations between people, and this object gets perverted if you can only be friendly to dogs or if you can love only people who abuse you. Or curiosity: its object is to secure knowledge of the world, knowledge that will be useful and enriching, but this impulse can be perverted into an interest merely in gossip about soap-opera celebrities.

In each of these cases then we have the idea of a human drive or impulse that naturally aims at something fairly definite but can be deflected from this aim into something more or less unsatisfactory for the person involved. Here is where the notion of sexual perversion is to be located. It is the idea that it is possible for sexual striving to go astray, to be misdirected, to wander off target. The question now is: what kinds of act, if any, are like this?

Suppose a person's sexual interest was aroused only by stereos or spiders or dollar bills: these were the objects with which the person wanted sexual contact, not human bodies at all. Wouldn't this be a clear diversion of the sex drive from its 'proper use', since the objects in question are not things with a sensual nature of their own? And isn't it also clear that, given human nature, sexual contact with these items could never have the kind of richness that sexual contact with another person has? Don't you think that, if this person were your friend, you would counsel therapy to try to bring a measure of normality to his/her sex life? I know that if it were *me* with these odd compulsions I would seek help if I thought I could get any – and not because I am a particularly conventional kind of fellow. We would think that the spider-fancier was missing out, that there must be some strange story behind his/her preference, that he/she can't be very happy being like that. The case is analogous to the cases of food and friendship and curiosity. It is not that we should come down heavily on such a person, flaying them morally; it is just that their means of acting out their sexual needs are, to put it mildly, on the wayward side. Spiders, stereos and dollar bills are being treated *as if* they were persons, because of some psychological quirk. Hence we can say that the sexual drive is being inappropriately directed, i.e. perverted.

I take it most of my readers won't take much exception to what I have just said about those hypothetical perversions. But what about the acts I listed to start with? Let me be brief here, leaving it to the reader to fill in the blanks. I hope it is clear enough to begin with that, on the suggested criterion, homosexuality does *not* count as a sexual perversion. This is simply because that kind of sexual desire is directed at the sensual nature of another whole person – it is just that the person happens to be of the same sex as the person with the desire. It was thus quite wrong to list homosexuality along with (certain) other items on my hypothetical list.

As to masturbation, I don't brand it as perverted either, since it certainly involves a relation to a person – yourself – but I do think that if someone can *only* enjoy sex in this way then there is something amiss with her, especially if there isn't even the thought of another in the picture. And it is much the same story for the other items on my list. If a man can only enjoy fellatio with a woman, then there is something funny somewhere, since he is not responding to her whole nature as a sensual being – he is sexually tunnel-visioned. And if a woman loses sexual desire once the plane lands, we are entitled to wonder whether it was the *man* she was really aroused by while up in the air. And so on.

I think each of us is pretty well aware of the content and structure of our sexual desires and can see how elements in this complex relate to each other; and I think we generally appreciate that certain elements in this structure shouldn't be allowed to take on a life of their own, squeezing out the rest. The focus must remain on the other person as a complete sensual being, and not shift to something that lies to the side of the person, or is a mere part of him, or is quite impersonal. No doubt there is no unique sexual structure common to everyone, and it is a subtle matter how the elements hang together, but we have a sense of what it would be to distort this structure, for it to swing out of balance. Roughly, this is when there is no engagement with another person *qua* person. Or, to put it less high-mindedly, when you are not giving your all to his/her all. Practically speaking, cover all the bases.

I am by no means advocating an attitude of harsh intolerance towards sexual perversions, no matter how weird they may seem. I am simply saying that the idea is not empty – on the contrary, it is a useful idea to keep in our psychic dictionaries. Its most benign role is in self-monitoring, not in the persecution and ridicule of others. On balance, I think the idea has been used far too heavy-handedly and indiscriminately in the past, often causing great unhappiness to people branded as perverts. The basic rule should still be 'Do what you want so long as no one else suffers thereby', but we should also bear in mind that not everything we want, in a sexual way, may be what we should want, given our true sexual nature. If electric toasters are the only things that turn you on, then it might be wise to examine your present inclinations with a critical eye. Just a thought.

That was a fairly difficult subject to deal with; prostitution and promiscuity are somewhat easier. What, to begin with, is prostitution? Simple: one person paying or rewarding another for having sex with him, where the paid person wouldn't agree to sex otherwise. This definition includes, of course, homosexual prostitution as well as heterosexual, and it may range from the stereotypical street hooker to the wife (or husband) who accepts material comforts for sex she (or he) would prefer not to have. Essentially it involves a kind of purchase, an economic transaction. It is having sex for the sake of a reward that goes beyond merely the pleasure of having sex itself. Now, is it wrong to buy and sell this service? Is sex the kind of thing that it is immoral to treat economically? I can sell you my philosophical services (I am doing it now), but can I sell you my sexual services?

Let us put aside the complicating question of the poverty and pressure that so often go with prostitution, so that we don't have the additional issue of whether people should be reduced to this kind of economic desperation, important as that question is. We will assume, then, that the prostitute could survive well enough without selling his sexual services, say by working in a factory or a pizza parlour or a bank. He is a prostitute by choice, perhaps because he can earn more this way and work shorter hours. Then: is his job immoral?

If it is, this can't be because he wouldn't want to perform the service unless he were being paid for it, since that is true of a very large number of ordinary jobs. So it must be something about sex in particular that makes it wrong to buy and sell it as a personal service. But what?

Suppose A wants to have sex with B today but B doesn't particularly want to. However, B knows that he *will* want sex with A tomorrow rather strongly, but that then A won't be so keen. Problem. Neither of them will have sex on either day if each goes by his negative inclinations. Sharing this knowledge, A and B hit on the plan that they have sex both today and tomorrow, so that A will get what he wants today and B will get what he wants tomorrow – the price being that both will have to have sex on days on which they don't particularly want it. In effect what A and B have done is strike an economic bargain in which each buys sex from the other in exchange for sex. We can imagine such a bargain being struck even within a conventional marriage. In essence then this is a kind of prostitution – a reward is given for offering sex that would not otherwise be offered. This is a less than ideal way of managing your sex life, undoubtedly, but it doesn't seem immoral (or imprudent) by any clear standard. It was a voluntary transaction designed for the mutual benefit of both parties, like many another transaction.

Now consider this case. A young man down on his luck needs money to buy food and can't obtain it legally. A sexually desirous widow wants sex and can't get it in the usual way, perhaps because in her society widows are condemned for entering into normal sexual relationships with men. She offers the young man money to have sex with her and he accepts, though he would have declined if he hadn't been so hungry. They fulfil their agreement and both go away better off than they were before. Again, this is not an enviable position to be in for either party, and one wishes neither had been pushed to it, but it is hard to see why either of them should be blamed. They both acted freely in their own interests and no harm came to anybody – indeed, there was mutual benefit. It may be sad and regrettable, but it would be a hard puritan heart that condemned this coupling couple. For he might have starved otherwise, and she might have fallen into a suicidal depression. Thus prostitution isn't invariably wrong.

The badness of prostitution, as it most commonly exists, is really just an instance of a wider evil, and results less from the essence of prostitution than from the socio-economic context in which it usually occurs. Prostitution often stems from poverty and despair, particularly afflicting women, and runs risks of violence, disease and exploitation. None of this is good, but it is accidental to the very nature of prostitution as an economic contract. Acts of prostitution have to be evaluated case by case, and not by the simple citation of a general rule, as the examples above illustrate.

Finally, promiscuity – having 'indiscriminate' sex with a lot of different people over a given period of time (not to be confused with orgiastic sex – having it with a lot of different people at the *same* time).

How many is 'a lot'? Opinions no doubt differ, but I suppose almost everyone would agree that a new partner each day for a year counts as promiscuity if anything does. Is this a bad thing? Or is it merely enviable? Some would say that it can't be a bad thing if done voluntarily and without deception and risk of disease. Others would insist that one partner per lifetime should be the limit (you can have another one only when you are reincarnated).

My own view mirrors what I said about perversion. What do we think of someone who sincerely claims to fall in love with a new person daily, happily discarding the love of the previous day? What about the person who says he has thousands of 'close friends'? We tend to think such people have their emotional register wrongly set, even that they can't really be serious. Genuine love must last longer than twenty-four hours and real friendship can't extend to everyone you meet. Sexual desire strikes me as rather like that. How can you *really* desire someone today if the next day you simply aren't interested, and not for any special reason? And not just every now and then, but systematically, over a long period of time. I mean, if you never sexually desire a person for longer than a certain minimum amount of time – even ten minutes! – then it becomes unclear what kind of feeling you had to begin with. A radically promiscuous individual seems to lack one of the key components of normal sexual desire: indeed one of the things that gives sex its special intensity – the focus on a single person for a reasonable period. Maybe this period can be quite brief sometimes, and no doubt people vary in how long it can last; but below a certain limit, and if it is ingrained, temporary sexual desire can't be full sexual desire – it can't be real sexual passion. Or so it strikes me. If you just can't desire a single person for longer than a day, say, then it seems as if your desires lack some kind of authenticity. You are like a person who can't retain an interest in any one subject for longer than a week, and who takes up one enthusiasm after another, only to tire quickly of each one and move restlessly on to another. This is a person who is never *really* interested in anything, in whom the 'interest-drive' is shallow and unauthentic. This may be why, ironically enough, compulsively promiscuous people are often not really interested in *sex* at all, but use sex to satisfy some other need, such as the need for intimacy or excitement or parental disapproval.

*

Sex is a subject on which strong moral opinions often go with a notable lack of rational support. It is also an area in which you have to be careful that your own preferences and biases and hang-ups don't lead you to prescribe courses of action for other people that don't fit them at all. Sex is the original home of taboo morality. But in rejecting taboo sexual morality there is also a danger of going too far in the opposite direction, just in order to distance yourself from the irrational and narrow-minded. I hope I have succeeded in avoiding both traps in this chapter. But I wouldn't be amazed if I hadn't.

6

Drugs

What is a drug? This is a trickier question than you might at first
suppose. Aiming for maximum generality, we could try saying
that a drug is a chemical substance that affects the body or mind
in some specific way. This is hardly a watertight definition,
however, because food would count as a drug if this definition
were taken strictly and literally, foods being chemical substances that affect body and mind. So would air, so would the
smell of garbage, so would acid on the skin. Drugs must then be
a special sub-class of such chemical substances. We need to
include in this class the kinds of medicinal drugs produced by
pharmaceutical companies as well as the kinds that are sold in
the park or on the street corner. Some of these drugs are legal
and some are illegal, and some of the legal ones are often sold
illegally. The kind that are illegal are nearly always the kind that
are designed to act chiefly on the mind, though of course there
are also legal drugs that have a mental effect – the kind psychia-
trists regularly administer. Some legal drugs have no known
medical purpose – tobacco and alcohol are obvious examples.
The common aspirin has a medical purpose and a mental effect,
namely to relieve pain, and it is legal everywhere for everyone.
Crack cocaine, on the other hand, is both illegal and medically
useless.

Taken together then, there are an enormous number of
different kinds of drug, with varying purposes and effects, some
working on the body, some on the mind, some of them legal,
some illegal, some beneficial, some harmful. Given this great

variety, it is unlikely that any interesting set of moral questions will be raised by drugs in general, and I have no intention of discussing every such substance in this chapter. My concern will be with a limited class of drugs: namely the kind that have non-medical effects on the mind, both legal and illegal. That is, I am interested in what are called 'recreational' drugs – drugs people take for fun or distraction or stimulation rather than those they ingest to cure an illness. Examples would be: nicotine, alcohol, pot, cocaine, heroin, LSD, glue, pep pills.

We can divide these into three groups: the stimulants, the narcotics, and the hallucinogens – though it is possible for the same substance to have more than one of these properties. Thus, some drugs perk you up, keep you awake, make you hyperactive – the stimulants; others make you drowsy and lethargic – the narcotics; and others make you see and hear things that aren't there, changing your perceptual responses – the hallucinogens. Alcohol, for instance, typically starts by perking you up, then makes you sleepy, and if you drink enough of it you have hallucinations. People ingest drugs of these kinds because they want to bring about one or more of those effects. They wish to alter their state of mind in some way by letting these chemicals act on their brains. That is the essence of the kind of action whose morality and wisdom we must investigate.

Now I am not a doctor or a social worker, nor am I very knowledgeable about the medical and other details regarding particular drugs – how dangerous they are, how addictive, how expensive. So you won't find many interesting facts about drug-taking in this chapter. My concern will be with the more general ethical and personal issues raised by drug-taking. I think there is a lot of confusion and unclarity about the basic questions of principle surrounding drugs, and my aim is to introduce some order into the subject, by providing ways of thinking about it that can feed into practical decisions in particular cases. My discussion will have two main parts: first, the questions of moral and personal choice raised by drug-taking; second, the issue of whether recreational drugs should be legal or not.

First, then, is it immoral to take drugs? Is it immoral, that is, to ingest a chemical substance into your body that changes your mental state in certain desired ways? And if it is not exactly 'immoral', is it a bad idea for some other reason? This question has an easy answer when we focus on the effects that drug-taking may have on *other* people, as distinct from those on the drug-taker herself. If these effects on others are harmful, possibly fatal, certainly it is immoral to ingest substances that have these effects – it is a form of gross negligence or irresponsibility. When a person gets drunk and then drives a car his loss of control becomes very dangerous and can easily lead to killing someone: so, yes, it was immoral of him to get drunk if he was intending to drive. Likewise if you know that a certain drug is highly addictive and also very expensive, so that you won't be able to support your habit without resorting to theft, and yet you knowingly get yourself addicted to that drug, thus embarking on a life of crime, then it was immoral of you to take it to start with, because of the harm this would predictably cause to others through your criminal acts. You shouldn't do what you know will cause harm to others. It is immoral for the same kind of reason that smoking in public is, especially around children, since smoking causes cancer, not only in the smoker himself but also in those who happen to breathe in the smoker's fumes. Thus drug use is clearly wrong if it harms others.

However, let us not exaggerate this point, since there are many things that people do that they know are likely to cause harm to others but which they feel few qualms about. For example, driving a car *sober* is likely to harm others, both because of the statistical probability of accident and the facts of pollution. You are simply much *more* dangerous driving a car drunk than sober, but cars are dangerous things no matter how sober you are, since accidents will happen. At any rate, no new or distinctive moral issue is raised by the harmful effects that drug-taking may have on others. It is just our old principle over again.

The harder question concerns the effects on the drug-taker herself. Suppose that taking a certain drug D has no adverse effects on others (this may or may not be a real possibility). Now there are two cases to consider: the case in which D has adverse effects on the user, and the case in which there are no such adverse effects. Adverse effects could include the ruin of health, a decrease in efficiency at work, addiction to the drug that produces obsessional behaviour, and so on. D might thus have adverse effects that counterbalance whatever pleasure is derived from it, or it may have no appreciable adverse effects, so that the pleasure it gives is not outweighed by the harm it brings to the user. Note that I am not concerned here with whether any actual drug can really have no significant adverse effects; I am concerned with the question of principle that arises *if* we consider such a case.

Now is taking D immoral in either of the above two cases? This is not the same as the question of whether it is immoral to encourage people to take D, by means of advertising or per- sonal persuasion. That question is fairly easy to answer in the case in which D is harmful to the taker, since it would come into the category of knowingly encouraging people to do harm to themselves – as with cigarette advertising. (A complicating issue here is that of censorship and free speech, which we shall come to in the next chapter.) And the answer is that it is indeed reprehensible to encourage others to harm themselves – though this is mitigated by the fact that people don't *have* to succumb to this encouragement. In the case in which D isn't harmful, the encouragement issue will turn upon whether it is wrong in some other way to take D. But my question is neither of these; my question is whether it is wrong *of me* to take drugs that harm no one but me and may not harm even me.

You might be thinking of sexual perversion now, which is a similar kind of issue. And you might be saying to yourself: 'If it harms no one else, how can I be *morally* criticised for it? It is my life, after all. It may be stupid of me to harm myself, if harm there be, but that is as much as can be said.' That is what you might be saying. And indeed, this is an appealing way to think about the issue, in terms of individual freedom. But the example of perversion may make us pause over whether that really is all that can be said. What we have to ask is whether drug-taking might be wrong in somewhat the way that sexually desiring toasters is. Does it show that there is something amiss with the psychology of someone who indulges in it? Is it the kind of thing that a virtuous person just doesn't do, no matter how medically harmless it might be to all concerned? Is there something warped or sick or distasteful about taking drugs? How would you feel if you found out that your mother does it?

To get any further with this line of inquiry, we should ask *why* people take drugs; then we will know what kind of motive it springs from and whether this a motive we can approve. Is it a motive that virtuous individuals have? Well, no doubt people can have any number of motives for using drugs: they might be curious about them, they might want to enhance their creative powers, they might be subject to peer pressure, they might like to flout their parents' commands. But let me focus on a common motive, which raises what I take to be the central question: namely, the desire to improve one's feeling of well-being. Is it right to take drugs for this reason?

People are not always in a good mood. They would like to be, but they are not. They may be unhappy because they have been left by a girlfriend or boyfriend; they may be poor and deprived; they may suffer from existential angst; they may simply be bored stiff. As a result, they do various things to try to improve their mood or at least distract themselves from it. Some people go to sleep, others listen to music, some watch TV, others munch junk food, some go for a jog, others light up a cigarette, some drink a whisky or two, others smoke crack, some take LSD, others sniff glue. When drugs are taken to improve a bad mood, then, they have the same kind of function as other means of making yourself feel better. Not that drugs are invariably taken to relieve a bad mood; they may also be taken to enhance a good mood. People often drink champagne when celebrating something especially joyful, or smoke a 'well-earned cigarette' after a strenuous game of squash, or snort some cocaine when a big deal comes through – just as they may listen to music when happy, or do some vigorous exercise, or dance, or have sex. In short, people do various things to enhance their feeling of well-being, and drug-taking is one among these things. Of course, not everything people do in order to feel better actually works in the desired way; sometimes they just end up feeling worse (I find watching TV does that to me). But anyway that is the motive: pleasure, happiness, distraction.

It would be a miserable killjoy who found fault with this motive, considered in itself: surely there is nothing wrong with wanting to feel happier, with seeking pleasure once in a while. The question must then be which of these methods of mood-enhancement are good and which are bad – and why. *Why* is it bad to snort cocaine to relieve depression about the state of the stock market but okay to listen to your favourite heavy-metal band? *Why* is being drunk all the time because your girlfriend left you worse than distracting yourself with overwork at the office? Aren't drugs simply nothing more than a quick and easy way to achieve a state of mind that you might bring about in some other more laborious fashion? Why not view them as just another piece of pleasure technology?

You might think that the distinction between the two methods of mood-enhancement is easily made: drugs are a *chemical* means of feeling better – that is what is wrong with them. But this is a superficial answer, because it is surely an accident that the characteristic effects of these chemical substances are brought about in the way they are. What if there was a particular combination of sounds that the human brain responded to in precisely the way it responds to the chemicals composing LSD? Or a pattern of colours with the mental effects and addictive powers of heroin? People would then get their 'high' by listening to those sounds and looking at those colours, without having to ingest any chemicals. Would this really affect the underlying issue? I don't think so. The distinction, if there is one, must depend on some other factor. It must be some other property of drugs that constitutes their difference from more acceptable methods of mood-enhancement.

I think the distinction depends basically on the fact that drug-taking has no value *other* than as a mood-enhancer, unlike other kinds of activity that are undertaken in order to feel better. It is, as it were, too 'pure' a method of feeling happier or deriving pleasure. It has no value in itself, for its own sake. Its value is entirely instrumental. So it is not like music or dancing or sex or reading a book or buying a new dress – for all these things are related to values other than merely that of improving your present mood. Let me put it this way. If a scientist invented the 'perfect drug', a drug that had no harmful side-effects, physical or mental, was non-addictive and always made you feel terrific, this drug would still be something that had nothing to be said for it *independently* of its power to cure depression and lift mood. It is not merely that it is just a quick fix; it is that it is *only* a fix. It is thus isolated from other things that make life worthwhile.

Connected to this is the point that drug-taking does nothing to get at the causes of the bad mood it temporarily relieves; so it is not constructive. This is as true of the tranquillisers (note the name) your doctor may prescribe as of the 'hard' drugs peddled in the ghettos. If you are depressed because you are not as good a ballet dancer as you would like to be, then taking a drug may relieve you of this depression for a while; but it won't relieve you of it in the way that becoming a better ballet dancer will. So taking drugs is, at any rate, not the same *kind* of mood-enhancer as those other things. Drugs are, as it were, *brute* mood-enhancers. That is all they are.

Still, we haven't yet said categorically whether they are good or bad. As with many other topics, there are two extreme views about this. One view maintains that it is *never* right to take any kind of drug, legal or illegal, for purposes of mood-enhancement. To do so is always a shabby, weak and discreditable act – something we should educate our children never to resort to. The other view adopts a hedonistic position, holding that if drugs give pleasure and relieve pain there can be no objection to them. The only objection can be that in the long run the unpleasurable side-effects might outweigh the pleasure of the moment. Thus, on this view, there can be no objection to the 'perfect drug'. The hedonist believes that the purpose of life is pleasure, that this is ultimately the only real value, and if drugs can increase the sum of human pleasure they should be encouraged. It is then, for the hedonist, a purely factual question whether drugs *do* increase the total of human pleasure. Ethically, the hedonist is in favour of whatever makes people feel good.

My own view lies between these two extremes. But it should

be clear by now that large differences, of a philosophical nature, divide the two polar positions – disagreements, indeed, about the nature and point of human life. In particular the issue of hedonism – of the ethical value of pure pleasure – lurks in the background of the debate. This raises conceptual and other questions. What is meant by pleasure anyway? Are there different kinds of pleasure, some more valuable than others? Might pleasure by itself not be a good thing at all? How does pleasure relate to other values like achievement and goodness of character? What happens when the value of pleasure conflicts with other values? These are all difficult questions, and are too philosophical for me to take up here. It must suffice to have connected the issue of drugs with these deeper questions – something that is seldom done.

What I would want to say, on a more practical level, is simply and unexcitingly this: it is all right to take some drugs some of the time for some reasons, but that there are other drugs that should not be indulged in at all, save perhaps for reasons of medical research. By and large the use of drugs should be avoided or restricted, but there are circumstances in which it is forgivable and even prudent to take them. I say this as a matter of plain common sense. Nor am I recommending anything terribly revolutionary in taking this line, because in effect this is more or less the received wisdom on drugs. You can take a tranquilliser if your doctor prescribes it and you have a good enough reason to welcome its effects. Some kinds of extreme depression justify this kind of drug-taking. But you must be careful not to let it become habitual and crutch-like. Similarly there is no harm in having a beer every now and then, even getting a bit tipsy if the occasion warrants; but don't let yourself turn into an alcoholic, and give it up if you find yourself with that tendency. As far as the other 'hard' drugs are concerned, from what I know about them (not much) they are a dangerous thing to get involved in: addiction, physical breakdown, crime, even death are regularly associated with them. Anyway, they seem to have far too much control over one's mind and will – and I like my mind and will to belong to me, not to some fizzing chemical.

In sum, then, there is no simple absolute rule about drug-taking: it depends on the drug, the person, and the circumstances. This is a disappointing result in a way, but perhaps it is useful to see that the issue is not the black-and-white affair it is often represented as being. Clearly, it is not good to be a heroin junkie, obsessed with where the next fix is coming from. But nor is it right to brand drinking wine with dinner a deplorable drug habit, on a par with crack addiction. We must respect distinctions, and be ready for matters of degree.

Smoking deserves a paragraph to itself. Here I must confess, shockingly, that I used nicotine for six years of my life – from age 9 to age 15. Yes, I smoked. I must have got through at least twenty cigarettes in those six lost years! Then the findings about smoking and cancer became known, so I kicked the habit (it wasn't hard). I also started coming under peer pressure to puff away in the lavatories at school, which determined me against it forever (it wasn't the lavatories but being expected to conform). Anyway, it is a foolish habit, and also an unpleasant and unhealthy one for the people around you. It can't be repeated too often that it is a major cause of lung cancer and other horrible diseases. I know that young people think it is cool to smoke: it makes them feel grown up, there is the thrill of legal prohibition, and no doubt it partakes of the fascination with fire that the young are apt to have. But the thing is, it is just not smart. Cigarettes are strongly addictive and it can be bloody difficult to break the habit once it has been acquired. Tobacco is the first thing to say no to.

I have been trying to take an unhysterical look at drug-taking, assessing its wisdom and morality, but it is hard to do this when many of the drugs that people are most prone to sample are illegal. This is because there are lots of good reasons, both moral and self-interested, for obeying the law, even when the unlawful thing is not itself immoral. Morality is one thing, legality is another. I have been discussing the issue as if all drugs were legal and the question is whether it is okay to take them as a personal decision – as if the issue were like hang-gliding. Needless to say, if the law prohibits a certain drug, as it once did alcohol in America, that in itself provides a reason for refraining from that

drug, since you don't want to go to jail and lawlessness is
generally a bad thing. But now I want to make a few remarks
about the issue of drug legality. This isn't strictly a moral issue,
though it involves moral questions; it is a matter of public policy,
of politics. So then: should all drugs be legal?

To say that drugs in general, or certain drugs, should be
legally obtainable is *not* the same as saying that it is moral or
sensible to take them; rather, it is purely a proposal about what
should be on the law books and be punishable as a crime. I think
it is immoral to betray your friends, to drink so much that you
can't support your children, to be intellectually dishonest, to
break promises: but I don't think any of these things should be
illegal. So it is perfectly consistent to advocate legalising something of which one profoundly disapproves. My question now is
whether the drug market should be legalised, not the question
of whether it is a bad thing to get involved in drugs, legal or not.

Of course, drug-trafficking *is* legal – at least in the case of
certain drugs. It is legal in large parts of the world to buy and
sell alcoholic beverages, and to drink coffee, and to smoke
cigarettes – I have even seen people openly scoring nicotine in
the street! So it is not really an all-or-nothing question. The
issue is whether *other* drugs, the ones people regularly take
illegally, should be made legal, after the manner of tobacco and
alcohol. As far as I can see, there are three main arguments for
this recommendation – one logical, one ethical, one pragmatic.
We will consider each in turn.

The logical argument is that the current laws are inconsistent
and confusing, sending mixed messages that leave people un-
able to settle on a fixed drug policy in their lives. Tobacco and
alcohol are legal, but pot, cocaine, heroin, LSD and the rest are
not. Why this distinction? People wonder, in particular, why it
is that strong spirits are legal and marijuana is illegal, given that
the latter is arguably less harmful than the former to health and
self-control. Why not make them all legal or all illegal? Or at
least try to devise some principled distinctions that render the
drug laws internally coherent? As it is, the law looks simply
illogical.

The moral argument is that people should not have their

personal freedom restricted by law if exercising this freedom does no harm to others; or no more harm than other potentially risky forms of activity – like driving a motor vehicle or doing construction work in public places. No matter that some of these drugs may be highly addictive, medically catastrophic, and totally soul-destroying: citizens of a free democratic state should have the right to do what they like with their own persons. As there is no law against suicide, so there should be no law against ruining yourself with drugs. It is a form of totalitarianism to interfere in people's personal lives by preventing them from ingesting whatever they feel like ingesting. One's individual freedom should not be infringed by government in this way. Where will it end?

The pragmatic argument is that the high incidence of crime associated with illegal drugs would be significantly reduced if they were made legal and regulated in the way other legal drugs are. This isn't just the trivial point that if you make buying and selling drugs legal you automatically reduce the number of crimes simply by no longer counting them as crimes. It is rather the claim that the most disagreeable criminal acts connected with drugs – the robberies, the murders, the crime gangs and syndicates, the corruption – would be diminished by taking the drug market out of the control of criminals. On this view, most of the crime connected with drugs is not a matter of the drug business as such, still less of the direct effects of drugs on those who take them, but rather of the very illegality of the trade, which puts it into the hands of people who operate outside the law, because of the enormous profits to be made. If the government licensed responsible vendors, as it now does with liquor sales, the drug business would have the same kind of crime profile that we see for the case of alcohol, i.e. relatively minor and peripheral crime. After all, we don't have mafia gangsters up to their old tricks now that the prohibition of alcohol has been repealed in America. Make drugs legal and the criminal aspects of the business will fade away, if not completely, then at least substantially.

These are all, I think, serious arguments, and a powerful case can be made that it would be best, everything considered, to change the drug laws in the direction of greater legality. But the question is complex and requires a fuller discussion than I can give it here. Let me just mention some of the reasons that might be given for questioning the above three arguments.

First, it is wrong to insist on total consistency in the drug laws, since drugs differ in their potencies and dangers, as well as in the extent to which they are integrated into other aspects of life. We shouldn't expect to have the same laws for beer as for crack, despite the fact that technically both are drugs. Legal consistency shouldn't be applied too crudely.

Secondly, it isn't so clear that the effects of drugs on people other than the user are as minimal as they may seem. Some drugs can lead people to do very dangerous and harmful things, especially acts of violence. And the effects of addiction on the unborn foetus can be terrible. Furthermore, there can't realistically be an absolute rule allowing citizens to do anything they want so long as the harm is only to themselves. We don't allow this freedom to people under a certain age, and there are cases in which the state has the duty to protect people from their own foibles. The enforced wearing of seat-belts or crash-helmets is a case in point. And if a drug should one day be produced that was powerfully addictive even after a single fix, and was generally fatal after just three fixes, and thousands of people were rash enough in moments of weakness to sample this drug, perhaps because of its remarkable power to produce elation; *then* the state would be justified in stepping in and taking this drug off the legal market – to save people from themselves. Sometimes state paternalism is justifiable, even where adults are concerned.

The pragmatic argument might be countered with the claim that drug use would only increase after legalisation, and that there would always be a large black market for drugs in the hands of the usual criminal types. Minors would still be sold drugs illegally, and the legitimacy accorded to drugs by legalisation would only stimulate more people to get themselves hooked. We might end up with a social problem much larger than alcoholism. Nor would the level of crime be held down simply by making it legal to buy drugs, since many addicts wouldn't have the money and would resort to stealing.

I think myself that the best way forward with this complicated issue might be to try a controlled experiment. Pick a relatively innocuous drug, say pot, and make it legal in one state or area, with the authorities handling production, pricing and distribution. Then wait and see whether health improves, crime falls off, and the whole thing levels out into something close to the liquor market. If that gives satisfactory results, try the same kind of experiment with, say, cocaine. Manufacture the stuff locally, so cutting off the usual criminal smuggling, and make it obtainable more cheaply from government sources than from street sources. Supply health care for people who want to kick the addiction and advice for people who start on it. Above all educate children in the facts of drug use. Then see if addiction rates improve and crime diminishes. If not, think again. You won't produce a *good* state of affairs this way, but it might be better than what we have at present.

The use of drugs of some kind is ubiquitous; we find it in nearly all societies at nearly all times. Alcohol seems to be the general favourite. The odds are that there will always be a 'drug problem', because human beings want to take drugs and are not easily deterred from doing so. This is a fact we may well rue but it is no good refusing to face it. What is needed is the best overall policy for containing the evils associated with drugs, suited to the specific conditions of the time, while balancing this against respect for personal freedom and tolerance for the odd gram of malt whisky. The problem should be viewed practically and humanely, not superstitiously and heavy-handedly. After all, it is human happiness with which we are ultimately concerned, not the demonisation of a bunch of chemicals.

7

Censorship

So far we have been discussing the morality of various kinds of deed – exploiting animals, killing the unborn, doing violence, having sex, taking drugs. Now we shall consider morality as it relates to words, and to other forms of representation; in particular, we must ask whether it is ever morally acceptable to suppress words and images. We have considered questions about what you ought and ought not to *do*; now we have to deal with issues concerning what you ought and ought not to *say*. Morality can limit your freedom to do what you like, if that conflicts with the interests of others, but can it also intervene to limit your freedom to express yourself verbally as you like? If so, is society entitled to prohibit certain kinds of speech? Is censorship ever right?

'Sticks and stones may break my bones, but names will never hurt me': so the old saying goes. Is it true? It is true that the mere utterance of words, however unflattering or cruel they may be, will never itself cause you physical damage – unless the words are spoken through an enormous amplifier that bursts your eardrums or something of the sort. A hail of hostile words will never cause you so much as a bruise. And this is worth bearing in mind if you are being verbally attacked. Unfortunately, however, words can hurt you in other ways. They can hurt you emotionally if they are spoken by someone you love and respect; or if you are thin-skinned, if they are spoken by almost anyone. That is, words can be effective weapons of emotional violence (see Chapter 4 on this). Given that, moral restraints concerning harm come to apply to acts of speech. You should not unjustly hurt others' feelings by saying things to them, as you should not unjustly hurt their bodies by doing them physical violence.

But words can hurt you physically too, though indirectly, if they cause people to do bodily violence to you, or to deprive you of your livelihood or liberty, or if they make people think ill of you in ways that matter to your well-being. Thus if A takes it upon himself to slander B to C, telling C a number of damaging lies about B, and if C believes what A says about B and takes certain actions that are bad for B, then A's words have certainly had the effect of hurting B through C's agency. More concretely, if one group in society makes, for example, continual racial slurs against another group, dinning these into the children of that society, then the result is likely to be bad for the group that is the target of these slurs. In notorious cases this can lead to lynchings and the like. So, yes, names *can* hurt me, especially if they are believed and acted upon by those who can do me harm. There is, therefore, a morality of speech. It can certainly be extremely evil to make certain sounds with your mouth, though these sounds do not themselves physically wound or kill anyone. There is nothing exculpating about the fact that mere words penetrate nobody's skin, since they can cause things to happen that do involve real violence.

It is precisely because of these familiar facts that we treat slander and false accusation with the moral seriousness we do. We reserve a special moral contempt for the kind of person who stirs up hatred and distrust between people – by telling lies, exaggerating, omitting key facts, betraying confidences. Since people are naturally inclined to believe what they hear, the verbally unscrupulous can always perpetrate damage to someone by mere words. And those who take the morality of words seriously always make a special effort not to utter things that may unfairly harm a person's reputation or prospects – not to speak of inciting physical violence against that person. I know that I myself reserve a special circle in hell for the slanderer, the malicious liar, the insidious whisperer of falsehoods – the Iago figure. Be on the alert against such people! Remember that words can be as morally weighty as deeds.

Thus it is right and good to practise a kind of self-censorship. You may not like Bert, for good or bad reasons, and you may know that you can damage Bert by spreading false rumours about him (or even true ones!), but you should restrain yourself from saying all that you could. And you should criticise others you see for doing this kind of thing: you should tell them not to lie about Bert, not to omit certain facts that put him in a better light, not to use inflammatory language about Bert. Gossip, of a sort, is all well and good, but it can too easily turn into verbal injustice. So watch your words. No doubt language has been a great boon to the human species, but it has also been a source of tremendous amounts of harm. In some respects, the speech-less species should be grateful.

In this sense, then, none of us believes in totally free speech, as none of us believes in totally free action. We think speech should sometimes be curbed by morality, that certain remarks are wrong and shouldn't be made. In certain cases, we may take steps to prevent such remarks being made, if the results are serious enough: we might threaten the speaker with a suit for slander, or even with a taste of her own oral medicine. Since words can function as weapons, very effective ones to a credulous audience, they fall under the usual rules governing weapons control. If they are used to cause unjust harm, they ought not to be uttered. They are morally wrong.

All this is at the level of personal morality – how a decent person should conduct herself with her speech organs. We have said nothing about questions of public policy, law, the enforced institutional suppression of speech. So nothing has been said in favour of censorship, as this is commonly understood. That certain acts of speech are immoral and should be condemned does *not* imply that the state, or some smaller social unit, has the right to apply the force of law in the prevention of such acts. To say that something is immoral is not to say that it should be unlawful. This latter is the question I shall take up now – whether censorship in *that* sense is ever justified. Should freedom of expression ever be curtailed by law? Could it ever be right to be sent to prison or fined simply for saying or writing or depicting something?

One view, common in liberal democracies, says unequivocally that free speech must *never* be suppressed by law. The only acceptable response to statements you object to, for one reason or another, is persuasion or exhortation or rejoinder, but never judicial force. There is an absolute and inalienable right to freedom of expression, which must never be compromised.

Three reasons may be given for this bracingly simple view: conceptual, political and spiritual. The conceptual reason draws attention to a distinction between the way words have effects and the way deeds do. I said a moment ago that people can act on words to the detriment of other people. True enough, it may be said, but notice that the resulting harm requires the active participation of the hearer of the words. The words on their own aren't enough; someone has to act, of their own free will, on those words, if harm is to be caused. But this isn't so with deeds like hitting and shooting: these impinge directly on the person harmed. So verbally caused physical harm depends on the collusion of a third party, who must accept direct responsibility for the harm done. You need a believer as well as a liar. The liar himself does no direct harm; he merely induces others to. But given this difference, it can't be right to treat the mere act of speaking, however malicious it may be, as if it were equivalent to the violent act it provokes. Hence there is never the same moral rationale for banning potentially harmful speech as there is for banning the harmful acts it may cause.

The political reason is that it is essential to the health of a society, especially a democratic one, that there be freedom of information – that people know what is going on in that society, especially if it is done in their name. The press, television and the other media should therefore never be prosecuted for publishing facts about what is going on, because this ensures that those who govern the society have some check on their activities. Governments shouldn't be allowed to cover themselves by muzzling the press, or else we shall end up living in a totalitarian state in which just criticism of rulers is treated as a criminal offence.

The spiritual reason goes something like this: the well-being of the human soul requires that it be able to express itself freely.

To constrain freedom of the spirit with censorship is to attack our very essence. This kind of reason is what lies behind the familiar insistence that the arts be permitted to develop in any direction they feel moved to, but the same point applies equally to the sciences – to the acquisition and transmission of objective knowledge. To thwart artistic and scientific freedom, suppressing creativity and truth, even punishing them, is a sin against civilisation, against our higher nature. Thus censorship conflicts with one of our deepest values. The creative spirit must be free, and its freedom depends upon our ability fearlessly to express its products.

Let me not beat about the bush about my position on this question: I believe strongly that freedom of expression is a basic and deeply important right, that its suppression is both morally wrong and socially disastrous, and that we must do what lies in our power to protect it. I have been exercising this right in these pages; and though some readers may not have liked everything I have said, I hope that you all respect my right to be free to say it – I certainly respect your right to disagree with me. So I am firmly on the side of those who, historically and in the present day, favour complete legal freedom of expression – artistic, scientific, political.

I do not, however, think that there is simply no issue here, nor that there couldn't be any *conceivable* circumstances in which restrictions on the right of free expression might be desirable. What I propose to do then is to consider a number of vexed areas in which some people have wanted to ban free expression, in order to see if a case can ever be made for this. We shall have to qualify the simple absolute principle stated earlier a little bit, but the essence of it will not be compromised. The areas for consideration are: political subversion, blasphemy, obscenity, and privacy.

There are people in the world (I have met some of them) who hold, perhaps only implicitly, that the state – any state – has a duty to protect itself from political subversion. If someone tries to undermine the state's institutions and laws, by means of speech-making and the like, they should be silenced by force. Such people take 'state security' to be of paramount value, and hold that if free speech conflicts with it so much the worse for free speech. And the same position is sometimes held in regard to social groupings smaller than the state – the club, the school, the family. These collectives have the right to do whatever is necessary to sustain their continued existence. Censorship is justified by the need for 'social order'.

I assume that few of my readers will share this opinion. We are now depressingly familiar with the manifestations of this attitude in totalitarian states (whose names I shall pass over in discreet silence): the control of the press, the secret police, the informers, the imprisonment, execution and torture of political dissidents. It is a point of view that cuts directly against the value of democracy, since it denies people the right to hear diverse opinions, and to arrange their societies in ways that reflect their informed wishes. Democracy and free speech are deeply connected values, which is why the suppression of free speech is a sure sign of dictatorship of one kind or another. Political subversion is in fact a *good* thing if it proceeds in this democratic way, since it is nothing other than informed political change. Free speech is the engine of social improvement; and suppressing it is a recipe for stagnation and worse. And remember, this holds as much for families as for superpowers.

But can we at least imagine a hypothetical case in which it might be justified to suppress freedom of speech in the interests of order and stability? I don't like the idea of this at all, but I think it has to be admitted that it isn't *impossible* that this would be the right decision in certain extreme (and unrealistic!) circumstances. Consider the following case. Imagine you are the leader of a large and prosperous country, in which crime is low and the people are generally happy with their lot. One dark and stormy night you are visited by the Devil himself, horns and all; you know it is he because he performs a number of nasty supernatural feats that no one else could. He has news for you, he says: actually *he* created the world, and he has his own devilish ideas about reward and punishment. In fact, he goes on, there is no God, just him, Satan, and his decree is that the good people shall go to hell when they die and the bad go to heaven. Thus he wickedly inverts what the devout have always believed.

If you want to avoid hell, therefore, the best thing you can do is to become as evil as possible as soon as possible. Murder, he says, with a demonic curl of the lip, would be an excellent start, preferably of the innocent. The reason he has come to visit you is that he wishes to make these delightful facts known to human beings. It has always been so, he says, but he now thinks it would be good Satanic fun to inform people of the true nature of the afterlife and then watch what they do to each other. The thing is that he needs you, the President, in order to make his message heard, since without your cooperation his voice is inaudible to human ears – he has to ventriloquise through your speech organs. So could you kindly arrange a spot for him on primetime TV so that he can spread the bad news?

Now you of course realise that the Devil's act of free expression will lead to enormous chaos and evil in the world, human nature being what it is, since people will start doing terrible things in order to be rewarded for their evil acts and to avoid punishment for good acts. Imagine the carnage! And it is in your power to let the horned one have his say and hence unleash that carnage. The question, then, is whether you have a duty in this case to suppress the Devil's right to free speech, given the results you know it is bound to have. What he says is true, you can see that, and all he asks is to be able to tell people the truth about their condition. Should you let him?

Well, my inclination here is to draw the line and deny the Devil his right to free speech, because of the enormous harm that would result and the manifest evil of his intentions. It is bad enough that evil acts are rewarded in the afterlife; you shouldn't make the situation worse by informing people of this. To accede to the Devil's request would make you responsible (we are supposing) for untold suffering and the total collapse of civilised life. This is a high price to pay for sticking to the principle of free speech come what may. No, I think I would tell Satan to go back where he came from. If he protested that he had a constitutional right to free expression, I would reply that this is an unforeseen exception to that otherwise admirable principle. I can't throw the world into total violent disorder simply in order not to infringe his right of free speech, notwithstanding the veracity of his message. Sorry, Satan, but that is my decision.

That was a far-fetched hypothetical case in which we might plausibly think that free speech has its potential limits. To my knowledge, no cases of this kind have ever arisen, so the principle of free speech hasn't been tested to the limit. Needless to say, this imaginary case shouldn't be used to justify the kinds of limitation on free speech that have actually been proposed on political grounds. A principle can be non-absolute without there being any realistic possibility of flouting it in practice.

Now for blasphemy. In this case (of which, in some people's eyes, my little story about the Devil may be an instance) I would take an even less compromising position. Here free speech should be inviolable. This has nothing to do with not taking religion seriously; it is strictly a point about what should be legally prohibited and what shouldn't. There are two kinds of case we might consider. In one kind, the speech act isn't intended blasphemously, and doesn't take that explicit form, but is rather intended as a joke about, or a serious criticism of, some religious tenet. In the other kind of case, the remarks are intended blasphemously, expressly to offend and wound the religious, and as an insult to God and his followers. The line between these kinds of case may not always be sharp, but it is usually clear what kind we are dealing with. It is the difference between accidental blasphemy and intended blasphemy. The first might occur in a work of art or theology; the second would typically issue from the soap-box of some opposed ideology with an axe to grind, or from a hostile mob.

Now my position is that the first kind of case is healthy and should not be discouraged. It may indeed be important to the life of a religion that people be allowed freely to criticise it or the way it is practised; nor should humour treat religion as strictly off-limits (so long as it doesn't go too far in the direction of intentional blasphemy). There shouldn't be laws against funny jokes or serious criticisms, no matter what the topic. Nowhere in the New Testament does it say that thou shalt not tell jokes about the Lord thy God; nor does it state that it is wicked to criticise any aspect of the Christian religion.

In the second kind of case, despite being an atheist myself, I do think it is wrong of people outside a given religion to make insulting blasphemous remarks about that religion, at least in the presence of its adherents. Religious taunts are bad. The reason for this is just that people hold their religious beliefs sacred and it is wrong to treat such beliefs with contempt or provocative levity. There are, for example, things you should never say about Jesus to a Christian – though there is room for debate about what these things might be. In certain respects, the case is analogous to insulting someone's race or sexual orientation or country or mother to their face. This is a nasty and deplorable thing to do – it is immoral.

However, however – that *isn't* to say that there should be *legal penalties* for this kind of badness. Certainly not violence, and not any other kind of enforced suppression. The right response, as I suggested in Chapter 4, is moral indignation, riposte in kind, withering contempt, public condemnation, sending to Coventry, withdrawal of friendship – all the ways we express our moral disapproval of a person's actions. But not imprisonment, not execution, not thuggery, not lawsuits and financial penalties. For that is to move into another area altogether – the use of simple force to prevent and punish the saying of certain things. This doesn't fit the nature of the offence, as well as being parlous from a moral and political point of view – since it infringes a right that we also regard as sacred. Where will such stifling of free expression end? If you legally punish the blasphemer, you will soon be punishing anyone who says things you don't like. Speech, however offensive and ill-willed it may be, should not be legally suppressed or criminalised. Blasphemy is just one instance of that general rule. Wicked it may be, but criminal it should not be made. People must be free to say what they like without fear of legal or violent reprisal. After all, words are just that – *words*.

Obscenity is a subject that gets people very hot under the collar. Let us focus our attention on pictorial pornography, the most controversial area – say, porn videos. Should these be banned? Should it be illegal to make or own them? This is not, again, the question of whether it is immoral to produce or watch such videos. It is a question about the law, about the legal right to free expression of a pornographic kind. Would it be immoral *of the law* to ban porn videos? Not artistic ones, mind you, but the frankly pornographic sort.

Let me begin with a key distinction between cases which seems to me not to be emphasised enough, especially where the pictorial representation of sex and violence is concerned. I mean the distinction between representations of intrinsically bad acts and representations of acts that are not in themselves bad. The latter would clearly include videos of people having ordinary sexual intercourse or any kind of sex not deemed intrinsically objectionable. The former would include depictions of cruelty, violence, rape, sadism and so forth – cases in which at least one of the participants is being coerced and abused in some way. (I don't mean that the people being filmed are *really* doing these bad things – though they may be; I am assuming it is all just acting and make-believe.)

Now it seems to me that these cases have to be considered separately, because they raise rather different issues. This is one reason why it is silly to lump together depictions of sex and violence as if they were morally identical. It is hard to see what could be so bad about representing something that isn't itself bad, but where you have graphic depictions of evil acts the question of the morality of such depictions must at least arise – especially if the acts are being celebrated or encouraged. So let us forget the former kind of case; only the latter raises hard questions of legal censorship and freedom of expression. Let us also agree, for the sake of argument, that it is wrong to make and enjoy such nasty videos.

Once again, though, nothing much follows about banning them by law. Depravity shouldn't be made illegal: people should be legally free to be as depraved as they like, so long as they harm no one else. No doubt depravity is bad – say, relishing depictions of the torture of children. But that isn't a good enough reason to put it beyond the law. Purely personal depravity should be each individual's private choice, so far as the law is concerned. Just as people should be legally free to imagine in their own minds whatever they like, no matter how appalling it may be, so they should be legally free to watch or read or hear whatever they like, despite its immoral content.

This is simply an application of the principle that freedom should be protected up to the point at which it adversely affects others. We should hang on to this principle even (especially!) in cases where it leads to activities we find corrupt and offensive. After all, *we* are not being compelled to watch the stuff. At most we should impose age limits so as to protect those not yet mature enough from exposure to what may harm them, psychologically or otherwise. So pornography should be treated essentially like smoking when it comes to young people. Part of being an adult is having the freedom to harm yourself if that is your decision; but children should be protected from self-harm. The important point is that the soul of each adult individual is his or her own business, and it is no concern of the law to try to regulate its state of inner virtue. That must be left to other agencies.

You may object that I am overlooking an obvious point: what about the psychopath who watches sadistic videos and as a result goes out and does horrible crimes? If such violence-causing videos were not legally available, the amount of violent crime would be less; so they should be banned for the usual reason – to prevent harm coming to others.

How good an argument is this really? It is certainly not misguided in the principle it invokes, but I doubt it should carry the day. One point is that sadistic videos would still be available on the black market, so the problem wouldn't be solved simply by making them illegal. Another possible reply is that there is actually no sound evidence for this kind of causal claim, as a general statement, and some reason to think that pornography might reduce crime because of the release it provides. But I don't want to get too involved in these kinds of factual issues, since this is an ethics book, not a work of pop sociology. The point I would stress is that the principle being appealed to here, even if it were factually correct, is one that gives uncomfortable results when applied consistently. The principle says that you should ban what is known to cause harmful behaviour in certain people, particularly the mentally disturbed – behaviour which would not occur but for the stimulus that provokes it. But is this a sound principle in general?

Let us grant that some violent acts might in fact be prevented by such a legal ban. The question is whether we are prepared to ban everything that is known to lead to similar harm. Cars would have to be banned to start with, since many harmful and criminal acts result from their legality, acts which wouldn't happen otherwise: this *is* a known causal connexion. Domestic arguments can lead to murder, with frying pans lethally deployed. Watching news programmes on TV can spark acts of violence, if they report events of sufficient moment. Poverty appears to be a large factor in causing crime. In the minds of the deranged, indeed, almost anything can cause outbursts of violence. Should I, a moderately sane professor of philosophy, be prevented from seeing a documentary about the evils of child abuse just because there is some maniac out there who responds to such material by perpetrating what it deplores? What if the violent imagery of the Bible, the torture and crucifixion of Christ and so on, had the effect on some warped minds of leading to similarly violent acts? Does that mean that the Bible should become a banned book, only available on the black market? Surely not. The mere fact that a text or film may have strange effects on strange minds doesn't look like a strong enough reason to keep these materials away from people who *don't* respond in that way. So the mere having of occasional bad effects isn't enough to justify making pornography illegal. For *lots* of legal things are known to have occasional, even frequent, bad effects in the wrong hands.

There is, though, a conceivable kind of case in which we might well think it right to ban a certain representational item, which mirrors other exceptions we have been compelled to recognise. What if the effects of a certain video were so extreme and so reliable that many murders were being committed daily simply because of it? Through some peculiar psychological quirk, a particular combination of stimuli triggers homicidal tendencies in otherwise decent human beings. You view this video and immediately find yourself wanting irresistably to kill the nearest person. It needn't itself be a sexual or violent video, just one that happens to have this kind of deranging effect on virtually everyone who sees it – because of some odd kink in the human nervous system. If, say, you stare at a film of a cactus on top of a TV set with the Mona Lisa in the background and hear a certain rare bird-song playing on the soundtrack, you go from Jekyll to Hyde in a matter of moments. Total frenzy!

Well, okay, if I were in charge, I think I would have this video banned by law, no matter how much people enjoyed watching it, and I would expect democratic support for that decision. The thing is a mental health hazard. But again, this is an extreme and unrealistic kind of case, the point of which is simply to show that there are *possible* limits on freedom of expression, not to suggest that we should, as things are, impose such limits on actual pieces of pornography. I would ban a car too *if* it were known to have comparably devastating effects.

So am I suggesting that, in the world we live in, there is never a need to restrict the free flow of information in any way? Should you be free to publish simply anything? Actually, no, I don't think that, because I believe there is one area in which a good case can be made for legally enforced censorship, though we have to be careful about how we define this area. I am thinking of forms of publication that involve violations of personal privacy. We all do things that we regard as essentially private, as not appropriate objects of public scrutiny; and hence we disapprove of people who snoop and pry. It is not necessarily that we are ashamed of these things and want to keep our public reputations spotless. It is rather a matter of what we feel belongs to that area of our life which ought to be ours alone. Suppose someone, say to make money, places a video camera in your bathroom without your knowing it. He films you doing all the things that are normally done in bathrooms. Then he sells copies of the film to people in your neighbourhood, particularly to those who have something against you. He even offers a public screening of you performing your bathroom acts. Imagine you are famous and that a film of this kind could have very damaging effects on your career and family and future life. Even worse, imagine someone building a mind-reading machine that could pick up every thought and image a person has in his head and broadcast it on TV. The machine starts broadcasting your inmost thoughts and feelings, many of which you would never express to anyone. How about that for freedom of the press?

(Don't scoff – it might one day become technically feasible.)

These publications certainly strike me as monstrous invasions of personal privacy. If they became widespread they would have very bad effects on the quality of human life. Here then 'freedom of information' conflicts sharply with the individual's right to privacy. I think that this kind of infringement of rights should be prohibited by law. The better surveillance techniques become, the more need there is for legal sanctions against violations of privacy. It shouldn't, for example, be legal secretly to film a member of the British Royal family giving birth and then sell the tape to the public. This isn't to suggest that politicians, say, should be able to keep their plots and deals, done behind closed doors, away from the public gaze, since these concern the public directly – they aren't part of a politician's private life. It *is* to suggest that the law may step in to protect those areas of human life that are commonly agreed to belong to the private sphere. By all means express yourself freely, but not by reporting publicly what I do in the privacy of my own home – or head.

Let me end this chapter on an absolute note. We have talked about freedom of expression, the making public of various events and ideas, either in words or pictures. While we have upheld the principle of free expression pretty firmly, we have also been compelled to recognise certain potential restrictions on the absoluteness of this freedom. But there is one kind of freedom, closely connected with freedom of expression, that I would be reluctant to compromise even to the limited extent I have qualified freedom of expression – I mean, freedom of thought. People should never be legally penalised simply for *thinking* certain things, no matter how disgusting or wicked or hateful these things may be. If a technology for effective thought suppression were ever invented, I don't think it could ever be justifiably used. What you do with your mind alone must never come under the shadow of the law. That way lies the destruction of the human spirit, the strangling of all creativity. It is violence against the soul. If anything should be free, thought should.

8

Virtue

Time now for a shift of viewpoint. The previous chapters have
dealt with questions concerning what moral views to hold about
particular concrete issues, and what to do about these issues. In
the present chapter, I intend to ruminate on a slightly different
theme, which may be my favourite: what kind of *person* one
should be. Not 'Which actions should I perform?', but 'What
kind of character should I have?' Of course, these two questions
are going to be connected, since you should *be* the kind of
person who *does* the right thing; but now I shall be focusing
explicitly on moral character rather than on moral action. I shall
ask what traits of character are the right traits to possess, and
what the traits to avoid.

In a sense, this is a more fundamental question than the other
questions I have discussed, because if we knew what made a
person good that would be a solid basis for deciding what actions
were right – they are the actions that flow from a good person.
Becoming a good person is a sure way of bringing it about that
your actions will likewise be good. On the other hand, probably
the best way of improving your moral character, or anyway
finding out what this would consist in, is to consider particular
moral questions, so as to arrive at the moral truth about them
and establish important moral principles. What is needed,
ideally, is a combination of both inquiries: an inquiry into the
right actions and beliefs in particular areas, and an inquiry into
the sort of person who will naturally do those things and form
those beliefs. A general moral tract, such as this one aims to be,

94

needs both of these. In any case, our topic now is goodness of character, the virtuous individual, the kind of human being one should try to become.

Some readers may be wondering, sceptically, why they should bother to be virtuous at all. Why not be a bad person? What *reason* is there for being a good person? The answer is, there is no reason – or no reason that cuts deeper, or goes further, than the tautology 'because goodness is good'. The reason you should be virtuous and not vicious is *just* that virtue is virtue and vice is vice. Ultimately, what you get from virtue is simply...virtue. Virtue may also get you health, wealth and happiness, but there is certainly no guarantee of that – definitely not – and in any case that isn't the *reason* you should be virtuous.

Logically, it is like the question of why you should care about your own future welfare: because your welfare is *your welfare*. Nothing more can really be said; and if someone just doesn't see it, there is not much you can do to convince them. It adds nothing to say that it is stupid not to care about your own future welfare. That is perfectly true, but it is stupid simply because...you should care about your own future welfare. Analogously, we can equally say that it is immoral not to care about being a good person; but again, this really boils down to repeating ourselves – it is immoral because being a good person is something you should be. 'Stupid' goes with 'prudent' the way 'immoral' goes with 'virtuous'. Moral justification, like all justification, comes to an end somewhere. At some point we have simply to repeat ourselves, possibly with a certain emphasis, or else just remain silent. Virtue is, if you like, its own justification, its own reason: you can't dig deeper than it. To the question 'Why should I care about others as well as myself?' the best answer is another question: 'Why should you care about yourself as well as others?' In the case of the latter question, the right reply is, 'Because you are a person to be taken into account too'; and in the former case, the right reply is, 'Because *they* are persons to be taken into account too.' To insist that I am me and they are them is merely to utter an unhelpful tautology, which does nothing to show that I have a reason to be self-concerned but no reason to be moral. People (and animals) have intrinsic value, so you should take them into account – which is to say that you should be good. Why? Because…people (and animals) have intrinsic value and should be taken into account – which is to say that you should be good. End of story. End of match. Good is good and bad is bad – that is all you need to know.

Or not quite all. Although virtue can't be justified in other terms, specifically not in terms of self-interest, it does connect with other values in ways that aren't just accidental. Beauty and truth are often linked with goodness as the supreme values: these three commodities are what the world should contain more of. I am happy to go along with these noble sentiments, but I would also add that beauty and truth are bound up with goodness in inextricable ways, as follows.

A good person is a truthful person: habitual deceivers are not good. And truthful not only to others but to themselves: they seek out and respect the truth for their own consumption, not fooling themselves about where the truth lies. She who loves goodness also loves truth.

Less obviously, beauty has a close relation to goodness. Many beautiful works of art are suffused with moral goodness, in ways that are hard to disentangle from their beauty; but more to the point, goodness of character is itself a form of beauty – what we might call 'moral beauty' or 'beauty of soul'. The character of a good person gives aesthetic pleasure. A bad person, by contrast, has an ugly character, a soul we find it repugnant to gaze upon. I think this is why we like to hang the pictures of those we admire, while we find it hard to stand the sight of the wicked. Thus goodness partakes of beauty. Indeed, given that not everyone can be physically beautiful, goodness of character affords one of the few other ways of exemplifying beauty. Nor does it require special talents or great labour, like being musically or poetically gifted. In a sense anyone can be morally beautiful, though not anyone can exhibit musical or literary beauty. This is because moral beauty is more an affair of the will than other kinds. So if you want to make up for a lack of looks, you don't have to become an opera singer: you can simply become a decent human being. (Me, I play the drums.)

This link between goodness and beauty is often noted in regard to the human face. The face of a good person is apt to radiate the virtue within, thus acquiring a beauty it would not otherwise have; while the face of a bad person will tend to reflect the inner ugliness and be repellent to the gaze. Look at the expression on a face, notably when in repose: it can say a lot. This is not of course a simple matter of plain physical ugliness being the measure of a man's badness – far from it. It is a much subtler thing than that, though one that most people can recognise when they see a clear instance of it (I mention no names). A physically ugly face can give off moral beauty, and a physically beautiful face can be marred by inner corruption. Nor, of course, is it easy to judge a person's character from her face, and major mistakes can be made, but with experience it is a skill that can be developed. Attend to the smile, the play of the eyes, the indefinable aura of the overall expression. Naturally the older a person gets, so that their face has had more time to mould itself to their soul, the easier it becomes to read their character from what begins at the neck and ends at the crown. I often think that a certain sort of tightness in the face is a suspicious sign. Oscar Wilde's novel, *The Picture of Dorian Gray*, is precisely a study on the theme of face and character. In it a beautiful young man's evil acts are registered horribly on his portrait, while his own face retains its youthful charm and innocence. In the end, when his conscience catches up with him and he destroys the portrait, his real face turns into the hideous face in the picture – a poetically just conclusion. So, if you are still wondering what reason you have to be virtuous, there is this reason at least: you don't want to end up looking even less attractive than you do now!

So let us grant that we should be virtuous; that still doesn't tell us how much effort we should put into the project. How big a deal is virtue, comparatively speaking? How important is it to develop a good moral character, relative to all the other things you can do in life? Should it be at the top of your list of priorities, or third, or tenth?

I think there should be room for some individual variation here. People differ in their talents, motivations and ambitions.

Some people will naturally give more of their time to moral activity than others; their lives will be more centred around ethical concerns. Doctors and welfare workers and politicians are (supposed to be!) like this: it is part of their job description to do good for others. There are those indeed who devote their lives to virtue, doing little else than cultivating it and its products. We sometimes call them 'saints' and admire them, rightly so. They may become monks or nuns, renouncing all worldly interests; or they may spend their lives helping the sick and poor without having any religious affiliation. For such people ethical concerns are paramount (I am not saying there are no hypocrites among them).

Other people may have special talents in the arts or sciences, finding their interests consumed by these fields. They will naturally devote their primary energies to giving these talents expression, with little time left over for moral enterprises. Others simply like to have a good time, to enjoy themselves, to do lots of fun things. These good-timers don't reject morality, but it is not at the centre of their interests and desires. Yet others are taken up with sport, finding everything else wan. And, of course, people can be mixtures of each of these extreme types. You might be someone whose main delight is playing the guitar, but you are very concerned about ecological issues, enjoy the odd game of tennis, and aren't averse to a couple of drinks with friends at the weekend.

My view is that each person must decide for himself, in good conscience, what kind of person he is and allot his time and energy proportionately, always remembering that there is no excuse for outright badness. There is no imperative to make virtue your central preoccupation; you don't have to drop everything else in a supreme effort to be good. Most people find it natural to act from a variety of motives: they want to achieve something in their lives, whatever that may be; they want to have some fun; and they want to be virtuous. They would like to do something for others, but they also want to do something for themselves. Virtue should operate in all activities, it goes without saying, but I don't think it should wholly supplant other motives. The full variety of human desires shouldn't be sacrificed to the moral motive alone. A human life is, or should be, big enough for a bit of each.

Where conflicts arise between desires, as is inevitable, there is no alternative to balanced judgement and the admission that you can't have and do everything. I would say, for example, that a mathematical genius shouldn't be expected to sacrifice his gift out of a desire to help out people less fortunate than himself. Since I rate intellectual values very highly, I am prepared to see them accorded considerable weight in personal deliberations. 'Don't interrupt me now to help start the neighbour's car – I'm on the brink of solving a major mathematical problem!' People with different enthusiasms might say the same about the importance of (say) great sporting gifts – and I can certainly appreciate their point.

Fortunately individual moral progress isn't terribly time-consuming – you can almost do it as you go along – so there is not much excuse for neglecting it. We are not impressed by a corrupt business man who tells us he never had the *time* to become moral. Being good, at least within your chosen sphere of operations, is something that everyone should be able to manage. You don't need special sabbaticals in order to cultivate virtue in your actions.

There is no short-cut to becoming virtuous, obviously. You can't really take a crash course in it, as with a foreign language, emerging a saint with a diploma to prove it. It is not like slimming either, shedding the bad fat. Virtue arises largely out of one's response to what happens to one during one's life, as of course does vice. For all I know, there is a substantial genetic component to being good. In any case there is no substitute for hands-on practical experience – for living a morally challenging life. This is what makes a person either better or bitter. Reading about it isn't going to endow you magically with all the virtues you wish you had, even if the writer has them all herself – never a safe assumption. However, it may still be possible to focus on the right things by reading about it. I have certainly benefited (I hope!) from things I have read – from Jesus Christ to Bertrand Russell, from St Augustine to Arthur Schopenhauer. So what I am going to do is make a list of virtues and discuss each of them in turn, noting their relation to the corresponding vices. You can nod, or shake your head, as I go along.

Here, then, is my chosen shortlist of basic virtues: Kindness, Honesty, Justice, Independence – the BIG FOUR. What do they mean and why have I chosen them?

Kindness is largely the province of the heart. It is a matter of having generous feelings towards others, desiring that they not suffer, acting in ways that spring from concern for their well-being. A kind person is thus often said to be good-hearted. Kindness is close to compassion, but wider, since it includes not merely a reaction to suffering, but also informs every encounter with others. A kind person is solicitous of other people's feelings, tries not to hurt them, still less to hurt their bodies, and is distressed when others are in distress. A kind person treats the happiness of others as if it were his own happiness. An unkind person, a cruel or callous person, goes out of his way to make others feel bad, to bring them down, even to destroy them, in mind or body. He doesn't care if he hurts others. In fact, he gets a kick out of the suffering of others, especially if he is the cause of it. Their pain is his pleasure. Beating the dog is his idea of fun. His heart is stone.

A kind person is often described as *nice*, an unkind one as *nasty*. These are suggestive terms: we might think of kindness and its opposite as the moral analogues of two kinds of taste or smell – those which have a pleasant effect and those which have an unpleasant one. A nasty person in the room is like a nasty smell; and being at close quarters with such a person is like eating something bitter or off. But the presence of a kind person gives an atmosphere of freshness and sweetness, like a moral flower. You want to breathe a kind person in, absorb his niceness. A nasty person you just want to spit out.

Kindness is not the same as love, in any ordinary sense; nor is unkindness the same as hate. A kind person treats others as he would like to be treated, but this need not amount to love of others. It is a purer thing than love in a way, more a detached concern or respect for others. Love is apt to be more self-centred, more self-serving indeed. Kindness to strangers is kindness in its least diluted form: but you don't have to *love* the stranger in any real sense – you have never even met him before! Kindness is impartial and uncalculating, and not dependent on the vagaries of personal affection. It is the ultimate basis for civility and 'good manners' – treating others with decency and consideration, as if they matter, as if they *exist*. To be kind is to be generous and tender of spirit, not miserly and harsh. It is the healing balm of human relations, instead of the serrated blade. Kindness is good. People should be kind.

Honesty is simply the trait of truthfulness, directness, candour. The honest person wants her real beliefs and motives known. She doesn't want to hide behind anything. It is the opposite trait to deceitfulness, manipulativeness, corruption – the whited sepulchre. An honest person tries to be open and above board, so that the book can always be identified from the cover. A dishonest person is forever watchful in case his true feelings and intentions should slip out, so he has to put on an act to conceal what is really in his heart. This act often takes the form of excessive shows of trustworthiness, so that others will be thrown off the scent. Some people are highly expert in this branch of the theatre, and their dishonesty can come as a great surprise. An honest person, by contrast, is predictable and dependable, since he makes a point of letting you know where he really stands: no act comes between you and his real self. An honest person feels a powerful commitment to the truth, which pulls at him like a magnet. He can't *help* speaking the truth – it just tumbles out of him. He makes a bad liar, even when it is right (all things considered) for him to lie. But a dishonest person treats the truth as just one option among many, one way to achieve his ends that may or may not be the most effective. He uses truth, rather than letting truth use him. This can make him feel clever and powerful, not subservient to any value beyond himself. He is quite comfortable with falsehood; for falsehood is his constant companion. But for the honest person, falsehood gnaws painfully at the conscience, like a splinter in the soul.

This is not to say that honesty is 'always letting others know what you think of them'. That is usually cruelty masquerading as honesty, a vice calling itself a virtue. Unkindness and tactlessness shouldn't be confused with honesty, though honesty can sometimes require harsh words. It is not a form of commendable honesty on my part to comment on someone's disfiguring birthmark every time I see them. Nor is it a sign of my virtue constantly to let others know how stupid I think they are. Honesty needs a good intention behind it, and it must be tempered with kindness – which is not the same as soppiness or weakness. Nor should the virtue of honesty be identified with avoiding falsehood no matter what. If the Nazis are trying to catch an innocent fugitive in order to kill her and they ask you if you know where she is, then you are morally obliged *not* to tell the truth. Honesty isn't blurting everything out without regard for the consequences. You can love truth without broadcasting all the time, never mind who gets damaged.

Justice is a kind of fairness, of balance, of awarding what is due. The innocent shouldn't suffer and the guilty shouldn't prosper. Moral evaluation, and associated outcomes, should strictly follow the rights and wrongs of the case. A just person, therefore, hates to see the wicked victorious and the good downtrodden. Wrongful imprisonment, for example, stirs his moral outrage profoundly. He sees no excuse for injustice, no matter what pragmatic justification may be offered. Nothing ignites his anger so much as false accusation and unfair punishment. His compassion for the innocent is matched by his fury at the guilty.

Accordingly, the just person is especially careful in his own life to ensure that his moral judgements fit the facts and are scrupulously fair to all concerned. If he suspects that someone has done something bad, he doesn't rush into hasty and ill-considered condemnation, even if he might quite *like* to think ill of that person for some reason. He considers the facts calmly and impartially, not exaggerating or falsifying them. Only then does he come to a final verdict. But equally, he is not squeamish or cowardly about declaring his judgement when he has satisfied himself that evil has been done. This judgement will then have all the solidity and integrity of the process that led up to it. Since there is nothing worse, for the just person, than the issuing of unjust negative judgements, he does his level best to ensure that he is not himself guilty of injustice.

It is the same for the official judge in a court of law as for the ordinary member of a family caught up in a personal squabble. The just person will not allow herself to be swayed by bias and emotion and self-interest. She will steadfastly insist on the firmest principles of decency and fairness: accuracy, balance, hearing all sides, rejecting favouritism, making the punishment fit the crime. In particular, the abuse of power of any kind – from family to state – will be abhorrent to her. No matter how much she may personally dislike someone, she cannot stand by and let that person suffer unjust treatment. For justice requires us to transcend our personal feelings. It calls for a detached respect for moral truth, placing this before all other consider- ations. That is why it is often such a hard virtue to cling onto, because it can require us to go against our personal inclinations. It tells us to treat even our enemies fairly! For this reason (among others) it is a deeply important virtue to foster. A society without a firm commitment to justice is rotten to the core – as is a person.

My fourth cardinal virtue has a less familiar name than the first three: 'independence.' I want to stress its importance be- cause it is not always given its due. What I mean by independence is simply the capacity to make up your own mind based on the evidence and the facts, and not to be swayed by social conformity or threat. For some strange reason, most people assume that they have this virtue in abundance already – they do it 'their way'. But in my experience it is comparatively rare. What people really have is independence from *certain* social groups, often composed of their parents and like-minded individuals; look more closely and you see the influence of some *other* pressure group lurking behind their firmly held personal convictions. So ask yourself in a cool moment whether your prized independence is really what it seems to be. Are your opinions *yours*? (The case of animals is a good one to bear in mind here.) Anyway, I am talking about the idea that the majority might be wrong. To be virtuous involves not doing what everybody else does simply because they do it, since they might all be mistaken. Don't be a moral sheep, a yes-person, a don't-rock-the-boat artist. Decide for yourself! And I mean, *really decide*.

This virtue could also be called 'intelligence', but that is a word that has been rather spoiled in recent years. I don't mean IQ or scholarly aptitude – how quickly you can multiply numbers and how many long words you know. I mean what is sometimes called *judgement*, the ability to weigh a situation up, to see into things. The opposite trait is our old sparring partner, Stupidity – the kind of wilful blindness that leads people into rash verdicts and stubborn absurdities. Stupidity: simply refusing to see what is plainly before your eyes. Oh, how I wish I could put an end to stupidity! It and its fellow gang members: Prejudice, Narrow-mindedness, Ignorance, Fear. Not putting two and two together, ignoring obvious facts, perversely persisting in error in the clear presence of truth – do you know what I mean? It is hard to live with, isn't it?

People really should use their brains in moral discussions, instead of chucking them out of the window. Otherwise intelligent people can turn into virtual morons when right and wrong come up. It is almost as if some folks think it is actually wicked to use your head when doing morals. Reflex takes over, gut reaction, the herd instinct – the most primitive circuits in the brain. No thinking allowed! Kill the frontal lobes! Reason is put on hold, for fear of what it might come up with. Well, that tendency is what we have to avoid, and what this book is dedicated to combatting. I am actually proposing – heretical thought! – that you use your *mind* to think about moral questions, not your abdomen or spleen or even heart – nor yet your society or history or parents or friends. That way, I think, you will have more of a chance of arriving at the truth, truth being what minds are meant for. Thus I put independence as the fourth virtue on my list.

Now, these four virtues shouldn't be thought of as operating separately from each other. They don't sit in you in a row and each do their thing independently. In any concrete moral situation, it is a sure bet that each virtue will be called for, and that each may need to be modified in the light of the others. Kindness needs justice if it is not to be mere softness; and justice needs kindness – mercy – in order not to be harsh and unforgiving. Honesty must be tempered with kindness and regulated by justice. Judgement is what enables you to mingle and modify the virtues appropriately, so as to act rightly in any particular case. To be fully virtuous, a person needs, not merely to possess each virtue, but also to be capable of orchestrating the virtues together. He thus needs *thought*.

When the virtues are each possessed to a sufficient degree, and they work together in the right way, then we say that the person in question is *good*. When the vices are present instead, conspiring together after their own sinister fashion, then the person is... – well, you can fill in the blank as you see fit. Not good anyway: a blighter, a stinker, a rotter, a devil. The kind of person not to be.

You may be finding all this a bit on the sappy side. You may have an image of the virtuous person as a dull fellow, dutifully tending his suburban lawn, going to church on Sundays, doing what his mother tells him – a lifeless goodie two-shoes. In contrast, you may picture the 'wicked' individual as a dashing and exciting figure, going his own way, living life to the full, taking orders from nobody – a full-blooded human specimen, warts and all. These sorts of stereotype often lead people to say that evil is just more *interesting* than goodness, deeper in some way – that 'the devil has the best tunes'.

I think this idea is quite wrong and stems from a mistaken picture of the nature of virtue and vice. It is the propaganda evil puts about in order to justify its own activities. To me, the virtuous person is bold and attractive, often in the thick of it, frequently tormented and torn. *He* is the maverick, commonly derided by the grey men and women of society. The vicious person I picture as mean and crabbed, skulking palely behind closed doors, his mind a dead zone, his heart withered, hatching his petty and ugly plots, locked up inside his own narrow fetid world of resentments and vendettas. He is a coward, a manipulator, a dank-souled kill-joy. I see nothing attractive about him.

Nor do I see why badness itself should be found more interesting than goodness, from an intellectual or artistic point of view. Think of the evil of the Holocaust: it was routine, bureaucratic, repetitive, sordid, vile – a complete negation of life. Why should this be found 'interesting'? I suppose what people must mean when they describe evil as interesting is that it has a kind of unholy fascination – hence the morbid curiosity shown in crime and torture and war atrocities. But this kind of 'interest' is the kind people are prone to have in the maimed or diseased or simply dead: they peep out at these things from behind closed fingers, simultaneously repelled and gripped by what they are seeing. Well, maybe so; maybe evil does have this kind of morbid fascination. But that is no reason to want to get involved in it, to want to live an evil life. You might as well say it is more interesting to be maimed and dead than whole and alive! No, badness is boring and ugly, repetitive and repulsive. It is *depressing*. Its music is muzak.

I am going to round off this discussion of virtue with a list of moral maxims. After you have perused them, you might like to make up some of your own, by way of homework. Here they are, then, in no particular order.

If you want someone to do something, persuade them, don't make them

Always be kind at first, but be firm if your kindness is exploited

Trust people unless you have reason not to, but don't be surprised if your trust is betrayed

In matters of blame, think twice before you speak

Be critical but not cynical

Remember that there is a future, not just a present

Never allow the low standards of others to lower your own standards

Admire good people

Be wary of envy, in yourself and others

Don't forget that everyone has to die and everyone was once born

Don't confuse just criticism with persecution

Be truthful, but not in order to hurt others

Let the facts speak for themselves

Beware of the abuse of power

If you are not sure you are doing the right thing, ask a trusted friend

Remember that bad things have often been done in the name of virtue

First be honest with yourself, and then with other people

Never let injustice pass unchallenged

Don't make excuses for cruelty

Don't take from others what is rightfully theirs

Be kind to strangers, but not because you too may be a stranger one day

Don't allow your temper to do what your reason can't

If you can't sing, be happy that someone can

Don't insult where you can refute

Don't confuse independence with rebelliousness

Respect truth above persons

Don't despise the unfortunate

Keep your word

Apologise if you let someone down

Don't apologise if you have done nothing wrong

Don't let outward appearance determine your moral judgements

Be tolerant of difference

Be humorous, but not at the cost of seriousness

Don't think that what is right is always obvious

Let other people finish their sentences

Stare at yourself in the mirror once in a while

In this book, I have addressed a variety of different issues, chosen because of their practical relevance and illustrative power. There are many moral questions I haven't discussed: euthanasia, surrogate motherhood, divorce, capital punishment, charity, wealth – to name a few. My hope, though, is that I have said enough to provide a basis for thinking about such questions. I have tried to exemplify a moral attitude, a style of moral thinking, a *tone*. The issues I have discussed, often all too briefly, also raise many more questions than I have had space to consider. Again, I hope that the reader can go on to think about these for herself, armed with the skills I have tried to impart. Moral literacy, like other kinds, involves being able to handle new problems with the skills acquired in dealing with old ones.

It is important to be able to read and write. It is also important to have some mathematical proficiency. But more important than either of these is the ability to arrive at informed and thoughtful moral judgements.

Index